THE POEMS OF DOROTHY MOLLOY

THE POEMS OF
DOROTHY MOLLOY

FABER & FABER

First published in 2019
by Faber & Faber Limited
Bloomsbury House
74–77 Great Russell Street
London WC1B 3DA

Typeset by Typo•glyphix
Printed in the UK by TJ International Ltd, Padstow, Cornwall

A CIP record for this book
is available from the British Library

ISBN 978-0-571-34846-6

The image on p. 260 from NLI MS Acc 6207 Box 18 is reproduced
courtesy of the National Library of Ireland

FSC
www.fsc.org
MIX
Paper from
responsible sources
FSC® C013056

2 4 6 8 10 9 7 5 3 1

Contents

GETHSEMANE DAY (2006)

Credo

The one essential thing is for my voice to ring out in the cosmos and to use, to this end, every available second. Everything else must serve this. This is being in love with life.

Every voice is needed for the full harmony. God's tune. God's energy in me.

No more wavering. Take responsibility. Transform moods by work, application. Burn through the parochial states of mind. Art is the flame. Just write. Go deeper. Deeper. The answer is always to go deeper. Burn. Cut and burn away to the truth. And be set free. And keep two feet on the ground. Let me connect to the universe with my feet. And breathe easy. Amen.

found in the notebook in which
Dorothy Molloy wrote her last poems

THE POEMS OF DOROTHY MOLLOY

HARE SOUP

(2004)

Conversation Class

I redden to the roots when Jacqueline Dupont zuts
at my French. She cocks her ear and smoothes her coif and
sits me on a poof, settles herself on a chaise-longue.

'Encore une fois,' she zaps, and taps her nails and sips
her Perrier. My tongue is jammed, my teeth are in a
brace. Her hands fly to her face. 'Mon Dieu,' she cries,

'Mon Dieu, qu'est-ce qu'on peut faire?'

I fiddle with my cuticles. She checks her watch and snaps,
'Ouvrez la bouche!' Her forty clocks tick on, tick on.
Her cuckoos coil behind their yodel-flaps. Her
    grandfathers,

lined up against the wall, come every fifteen minutes
with a boing. 'Finie la classe!' She pours herself
a glass of Armagnac. 'Vous voulez un petit peu?'

I sluice the liquor back.

My tongue is loosed. My eyes are glazed. I sing
the *Marseillaise*. I feel a revolution
in the red flare of my skirt.

A Walk in the Forest

Electric fences hum in the forest of Fontainebleau,
disturb the twig and branch, the hand and hoof, the bristle,
and the silver-sickled tusk.

Birds avoid this place from dawn to dusk; the stags merge
with the trees. We lose our bearings in the labyrinth of leaf.
Hornets buzz around us

as we bend over the map. We cannot find the star-shaped
    clearing
where the five paths meet. I lag behind, I'm overdue.
I drag my feet. But when my waters

break, I send you forth to blaze a trail. I circle round,
ungird my loins, shake loose my hair. The sun goes down
    blood-red,
the fences spark; the bear moans

in the dark, the wild boar blinks. The night is hung with
    Zodiacs
and spiders, zinging bats. The wolves rush by in packs.
Deep in the earth I hear the vixen

cry when, doubled up, I stretch out silent arms
to catch the child that crowns between my thighs; I cut
    the cord
with teeth grown sharp as knives,

ingest the afterbirth.

Hare Soup

Monsieur Vidal is up at first light
with Kruger, his dog, shooting hares in the field
beyond where the vegetables grow.
He shatters the dawn with his gun.

Outside my window, ramshackle France.
Down in the foul-smelling kitchen, Madame.
On each page of my notebook, ahead of my scrawl,
the stink of the hare soup spreads.

At the stroke of *midi*, we sit at the table,
Monsieur and Madame Vidal, the idiot
Didier and me. I force down
the pottage. The gun-dog salivas my knee.

Didier kicks him aside, makes cow-eyes
at me. He calls me, in whispers, *coquette*,
his *jolie amie*. Sated with hare soup,
pommes frites and *compote*, black wine

and champagne, Monsieur and Madame Vidal
slump over their cups. Under the table
Kruger unsheaths his prick: a startle
of red, pencil thin, sticks out of his fur.

Didier swiftly unbuttons his flies.
He lifts up my skirt with his foot. He lunges
and tears at my blouse. I kick him aside.
When I stab at the O of his mouth with my little

canif, bouquets of old-fashioned roses
fall into my lap: petals shot with bright flashes
of scarlet and purple, vermilion, alizarin,
ruby, carmine and cerise.

Pascual the Shepherd

Down from the mountain pastures, Pascual, the shepherd,
binges at the bar.

He orders another brandy, in the singsong voice
he uses with sheep.

A young man comes in with his bride, in a flurry of snow,
to have one for the road.

Pascual raises his glass: 'Just wait till you bed her tonight
and you're snug in her fold . . .'

His tongue lollops and slurs. It cleaves to the roof of his
    mouth.
In the mirror a blur

of coiled horn rises out of his skull; and his eyes turn bright
    pink.
At the back of his head

he senses a movement of flocks; the slither of hoof
over rock, the bleat

of a lamb in the drift. Pascual shifts on the bar-stool. He
    gauges
the depth of the floor

with his fathomless feet and propels himself into the street.
Dogs howl

round his boots as he walks the tight rope of the cobbles.

Infant of Prague

I push him around in his pram. He is chalky
with lace, starched to his underskirts, taut
in his tunic and cloak.

He is ruffed at the neck, his heart hangs on his breast
like a plum; a crown holds his skull in its cincture
of gold. Flat

on his back in his princely layette, he clutches
his toy orb and cross. He fixes his gaze
on the lattice of silver

and black that comes between him and the sky.
He looks into my soul, sees the sixpence I stole
from my grandmother's purse.

He lets out a cry. I gather him up
in his ermine and scarlet. I lull him in Spanish
and Czech, brush the pale

of his cheek with my lips. Crimson embroideries
seep through his clothes; there is blood on my hands.
An ooze of vermilion

darkens the flax of his curls. Water flows
from the gash in his side. He is stiff as a statue,
his feet are stone cold.

But he glows like a little red lamp when he's back on his plinth at the top of the stairs. He revives like a Jericho rose.

Stigmata

On mammy's side
we were punsters and pugilists,
pillagers, prophets,
eaters of raw potatoes
and gazers at stars.

Mechtild and Hildegard, pray for me,
Francis, Theresa and John.

On daddy's side
they played roulette and Black Jack;
the one-armed bandit;
strip-poker, gin rummy,
cribbage and craps.
They went to the dogs.

Mechtild and Hildegard, pray for me,
Francis, Theresa and John.

As for me, I had visions
as soon as my breasts were in bud.
The Sacred Heart bled
on the mantel. A luminous
lady crushed snakes
with her feet. The Infant
of Prague came to call.

Mechtild and Hildegard, pray for me,
Francis, Theresa and John.

I lie on the analyst's couch,
my third eye ablaze. He tightens
his sphincter. He shrinks from my gaze.
I dig in my heels; refuse
to show him my hand: the strawberry
blood in my fist.

Mechtild and Hildegard, pray for me,
Francis, Theresa and John.

Ice Maiden

I walk in my night-dress and slippers
along winter beaches in Finland.
My earrings of polished tin
flash at the Northern Lights.
I shovel up the sea.

But the cold is quick. Quick
as I crack open the rock
of the ocean with my axe,
it freezes behind me.
My task is endless.

Family Circus

Dadda flexes his muscles. His buttons
go ping. His chest-hair springs out
of his vest. I sit mute as he lashes
at Mamma.

Mamma slumps in the chair. With her eyes
calls her infant performer, her stage-hand,
her prop. I stand firm in my sequins
and tights.

I make doe-eyes at Dadda; tap-dance,
do the splits. When the globus hystericus
swells in my throat, I swallow
my tongue.

Grandma's Zoo

There's a zoo in Grandma's pocket:
horse and bull, fish and bird,
stag, pig and rabbit. Hound.

When I stay with Grandma,
she takes an animal out of her pocket
and gives it to me:

a charm against the foghorns
booming on the pier;

a charm against the steam-engines
whistling in the dark;

a charm against the elephant-man
who comes bellowing to my bed.

'Was it like this?'

Beatrix cried
when a strange man forced his way
into her room, put his hand
up her jersey, his tongue
in her mouth, tore
at her skirt and gave her
a jolt. Blood on her shoe.

Beatrix cried
when she told her boyfriend
all about
what the strange man did.

'Was it like this?' her boyfriend asked.
His voice was strange. He pushed her hard
against the wall, put his hand
up her jersey, his tongue
in her mouth, tore
at her skirt and gave her
a jolt. Blood on her other shoe.

Beatrix cried.

Eternity Ring

I can't get this blasted thing off:
the ring set with stones that eats into

my flesh. I've tried fretsaws and slashers
and pneumatic drills; Fatima,

butter and soap. Lard.
I rode a tank over my knuckles,

I dropped a bomb onto my hand.
The ring is still grand.

'Long time no see'

I met Laura in the field,
looking pale behind her glasses.
Was she weeping in the grasses?
I met Laura in the field.

I was strolling in my wellingtons,
my anorak and woolly cap.
I didn't want her kind of crap.
I was strolling in my wellingtons.

She said, 'Long time no see.
He's gone again, that bastard Matt.'
I replied: 'Well, fancy that.'
She said, 'Long time no see.'

I could have said: 'He's in my bed.'
I could have told her, but I didn't.
I nearly told her, but I didn't.
I could have said: 'He's in my bed.'

I met Laura in the field,
looking pale behind her glasses.
Was she weeping in the grasses?
I met Laura in the field.

Small Wedding

They wanted a small wedding. Found a priest
who did it for a song. They gave each other
barmbrack rings; a pea, a bean, a stick, a rag;
a Christmas cracker joke, a paper-hat.

He wore a pin-striped suit with wide lapels
and ankle flares. She wore her polka-dots.

Her bouquet was a dandelion; his buttonhole
a daisy; the wedding breakfast, ice-cream
on a doily with a peach.

Jenny moved a mountain just to be there.
Stephen made a speech.

Floating with Mr Swan

Mr Swan, the anaesthetist, jabs at my arm
till I'm jelly-leg, head-flop and flap-wing.

He bears me aloft in his beak. He plucks
at my pubes. Kisses me on a mouth

that won't pucker or purse. My tongue is a wodge
of wet paper. My plasticene lips

don't belong on my face. My words are a slur of
'I wuv ya. I wuv ya.' He fiddles

with tubes, takes out his syringe. Then he rises
to meet me. Like Leda, I wait for

his thrust. All I get is a slap on the cheek
from the nurse with the upside-down watch

and the back-to-front hands.

First Blood

Après-dîner we sip anisette.
You tell me your stories of paradise
lost. I tell you of tennis-club
hops, Auld Lang Syne and a mistletoe
kiss.

Your lids at half-mast, you refill
my glass. I put on my rose-coloured
specs. I tell you of Antoine,
the bold boy from France, my heart
like a fizz-bag

when he squeezed my hand. How we danced
that last dance! Comatose in the dead
heat, you stare at your plate:
'Et alors?' I tell you of nibblings
in kitchens

at midnight, of shocking-pink lipstick
that glowed in the dark, the ultra-fine
mesh of my first fish-net stockings,
the mess of my feet in my first high-heeled
shoes.

I tell you of camisoles slotted
with ribbons, my first full-length dress
made of satin and lace; the mugs
of hot coffee, the Aga, the clothes-horse,
the starch

in my petticoat, the rouge on my face
when I felt the first frisson of fur.
You beat a tattoo on the table,
you 'psst' at the waiter to flag down
a cab,

push me back on the leatherette seat.
I am weak at the knees. Fast forward
and freeze.

Cut.

At the back of my head a camera
pans over the scene. Someone
is opening the door of my house
with a scalding hot key. There is blood
on the floor.

Someone is screaming 'For each one
you fucked'. Someone is calling me
'Whore'.

Black Flies

Sister Cherubina, lumpy
in her habit, rosary beads
snarling at her ankles,
scoops cold tea-leaves
out of a bucket.

Black flies on the floor.

Trapped on a high stool,
behind locked doors, I racket
at a grand piano; fingers slippery
on keys of blackberry
and meringue.

Black flies on the staves.

Sister Cherubina humps past
the music room.
I hear the bucket clang.

Mother Anastasia beats time
with her stick: raps me
on the knuckles.

Black flies fill my eyes.

I can't find my feet.

The Woman and the Hill

Clad only in oilskins, I ride a man's bike,
glide along with reptilian sloth.

Chin on the handlebars, a swaddle of hair
on my back, my comatose iids

are like lead. When I get to the hill, I dismount,
hide my bike in the gorse. I pedal

the buttery slope with my antediluvian
feet. For aeons I treadmill

in place till a ladder of roots pulls me into
the trees. I grow dark as the forest

slides over my face. I visit the sett
of the badger, the lair of the fox;

adore the wild sow on her altar of wood.
I slough off my skin. The wind gathers

my hair in its snood. From peep-holes high up
in the bone of my head, the eyes of a goshawk protrude.

Family Get-together

Only one little bitch can cross the divide
between us. Hands reach out

from separate worlds to touch her fur.
She can curl up on anybody's

lap. She gets the soft side
of everybody's tongue.

But lookie here. See these,
our hearts, come straight from the butcher's

hook. They hang on our chests
like rubies, wrapped in cellophane

and twine, with big red blobs
of sealing-wax to guarantee them

tamper-proof.

In the makeshift village cinema

The stalls are kitchen chairs. They're no good
for courting. The adults above on the balcony
watch every move.

We crack sunflower seeds between our teeth,
feel each other sideways through pockets
full of hands,

all thumb; shed our shoes, play footsie
under the seat. We talk back to the stars
on the screen,

smack our lips at the celluloid kisses,
crunch out at the interval on carpets
of husk,

escape to the street. The crash
of the river masks our sweet nothings
as we squeeze

in the dark. Jolted by the bell
for Part Two, we grope our way back
with red cheeks.

The voyeurs in the gods settle down
and the show must go on. As the amateur
usherette

fades with her torch, we resolve
to strip off this tight valley tonight
and make it

over the highest peak

                    into France.

French Hotel

We get there through the blinding fields of rape.
Dinner is late.
Pâté de foie gras, a piece of veal:
cold cuts
upon a plate. Dusty wine. Crusty bread.

Madame is pregnant; Monsieur is *en garde*
behind the till.
A serving-girl, too shy to speak, can only take
our order
for dessert. A trifling thing. *Compote.*

The rain drops on the corrugated roof.
The dark magnolia
opens up her cup beside the trough.
Insomniac,
the orphaned calves, the bonny-clabbered cows

with bursting teats, the honking force-fed geese
swirl
in my head. To while away the wee small hours,
I swat mosquitoes;
count the corpses on the blood-stained ceiling of this small hotel.

It's croissants, *comme toujours*, for breakfast; pots
of *confiture*,
café au lait. We check the etymology
of Fontainebleau.
'Belle eau', says the *patron*. 'C'est ça. Bien sûr.'

We bid a fond *adieu*. Unfold our map. Swear
we'll be back.
Drive south, as planned, to do the Côte d'Azur.

Near Sagunto

Splitting the curtain of beads, she welcomes me in,
her rope soles soft on the flags.

She speaks in a strange tongue, English a strain
on her lips after so many years.

Husband and sons dark as figs, her mulberry daughters
are silky as cats at her feet.

She has ripened in the heat. Except for the pile of bright
    hair
on her head and the blue eyes that hide

in the flap of her fan, she is Mediterranean now,
at home in their olive ways.

It might have been me had I stayed, strolling in spring-time
through acres of pink almond trees,

seeking in summer the shade of my own orange grove.
But

the north wind havocs my face. I no longer belong
in this place.

Tramontana

In Cadaqués the women with red arms and pickled hands
    salt anchovies.
The fishermen, marooned in bars, smoke fat cigars; play
    chess and dominoes.
The tramontana rattles doors and shutters. Waves crash on
    harbour walls.
The people here go mad. They blame the wind.

You throw logs on the fire; pine-cones for resin, sizzle,
    incense-rise.
You scrape the hard-wood palette with a knife, burn off
    old paint, toil
with your rags and turps. Half-faint, turn to the sink, pour
    in the bleach.
The people here go mad. They blame the wind.

The tramontana strips the beach of sand. The storks are
    gone. Gone the swallows
from their mid-flight resting-place beneath your arch. Gone
    south to Zanzibar.
I climb the steep steps to the terraced roof. A frieze of pines
    screens out
the white-horsed sea. Rough passage waits for me, as I go
    north.
The people here go mad. They blame the wind.

Stalemate

Because I swam nude in the sea on midsummer's night,
you sulked for a year on your bed in the Street of the Fig.

Now on the Eve of St John two thousand and one,
you and I, Baldomero, are still at our posts, daggers drawn.

Fool's Gold

You drew me naked as I sat,
my shoulders straight, my head held high,
my face turned to the light.

You took me in with narrowed eyes
when I lay down, half-hid in shade.
Your pencil caught me on the page.

You drew us fusing at the lips,
afloat above the chimney-pots,
my head flung back, my night-dress loose,

my bracelets glinting in the clair
de lune.

In Montserrat you pledged your troth
upon Assumption Day.
The flags, the stones, the dumb bells

of the ancient church bore witness,
and the silent stained-glass windows
wrote it down. And it was done.

Done.

I kept your promise in a pyx,
a bubble on a swizzle stick,
long after you had gone.

I keep it in a shoebox now,
fool's gold, protected from the light,
along with First Communion snaps

and rosaries with pearly beads,
and baby teeth the fairy-folk
forgot.

Sea-bitch

She softens in the sea. Loses the shape
of her clothes.

Always the black elephant swimming beside her.
The short-snouted porpoise

buttering her up. Blubbery as a seal
in salt water,

she lets me touch the purple jellyfish of her heart;
leaves her sting

in the melt of my hand. Sea-bitch, I have come half-way
to meet you.

Looking for Mother

I ransack her room. Loot and pillage.
I root in her trunk. Crack open
the tightly sprung boxes of satin
and plush. Pierce my breast with her butterfly

brooch. I pose in her hats,
French berets, mantillas of lace,
the veil that falls over her face,
the boa she wraps round her neck.

I try on her shoes. Her slippers
are mules. I can't walk in her callipered
boots. I break into her wardrobe.
Hands grope in the dark. Faded bats,

like umbrellas, are humming inside.
Stoles of fox-fur and mink: tiny claws,
precise nails. Lips clamped in the rictus
of death. I'm hot on the scent

of oestrus, umbilicus, afterbirth,
eau-de-cologne. I fling myself
down on the bed that she made
of dirt from the Catacombs, blood

of the saints. Under the counterpane,
nettles, goose-feathers, a torc.

Plaint

I've prayed with others of my ilk at Canterbury,
Compostela, Montserrat. In Walsingham
I've kissed the vial of Virgin's milk, the silky bones
of Madeleine in Vézelay, the Baby Jesus'
swaddling clothes in La Chapelle. And now in Chartres
I fast, and try my luck.

I kneel before the altar where *La Sainte Chemise*
is glowing in its box. Light a candle to the
Lady on the Pillar juggling with the flaming
hearts. The Count of Dreux salutes me as I
pass. The King of France looks up from braiding
Blanche's hair, and nods.

I don the pilgrim's conch. I beat my breast;
betake myself to Martyrs' Well, sink through the liquid
core of Holy Mountain, full eighteen fathoms
deep. Angels weigh my soul on scales
of air and lead and glass. I read the stars
and weep. I cross myself

au nom du Père, du Fils, du Saint Esprit.
The gargoyles leer. A donkey plays the hurdy-gurdy
on a plinth. Women heel and toe it round
the labyrinth. I follow in bare feet.
My blind soles catch the rhythm as they touch the black
on white. I go to Golgotha

and back. I count the ninety doors in this
Cathedral. I trace the masons' signatures
on stone. I find the steps, a thousand treads,
that spiral to the roof. Rose-windows spin
above the graven apse where Mary
births her baby in the cave

at Bethlehem. The Wise Men gather round with
precious gifts. The angels pause mid-flight.
Prostrate before the Child, I make my plaint.
The Virgin intercedes. She lets me stroke
Le Saint Prépuce. The marble bleeds.
I sing the great Amen.

Cast Out

She wears a black cowl round her head, her grey hem sweeps
    the dust.
She circles my walled city with her clappers and her cup.

From battlement and organ-loft I throw her food to eat:
unleavened bread, goat's cheese, the flesh of swine. But God
    forbid

she draw the water from my well or raise her lips to mine.
I fill my mouth with cloves. I hold my nose. I breathe into

a handkerchief of lace. All night I hear her pace.
I douse myself with vinegar, rose-water, eau-de-vie.

She calls my name. She rattles at the locks. She drinks the slurry
from the trough. She shadows me in dreams. I pray to God,

'Oh let it end. Enough!' She's shed her eyebrows, lost her sense
of touch. Her voice is like the toad's. The priests call out

'Leviticus, Leviticus'; perform her funeral rite,
as it behoves, beside the fresh-dug pit. The coffin waits;

the winding-sheet, the spices and the spade; the carrion crow.
I sprinkle her with clay, ignore her cries. I turn away

to ring the Requiem bell. She joins the living dead.
At Mass I see her lean into the leper-squint, receive

from some gloved hand the Sacred Host. Until Christ comes
   to rest
upon my tongue, I live in dread. My palace is a Spittle House.

I wear beneath my robe her running sores. Under my hood,
her face.

Lady of Sorrows

Knives in her chest,
the Lady of Sorrows
glows in her niche.

He has marched off again,
the little tin soldier,
banging his drum. Ratatat.

No kiss could detain him,
no love-bite on earlobe
or nape. There is work

to be done. Ratatat.
He blows hot down the telephone,
sends her a dildo from France.

She pukes on his pillow,
pulls knives from her chest,
throws the gold ring away.

He comes goose-stepping back,
a gun in his pocket.
Work to be done. Ratatat.

In the outhouse he plugs her
– love-bites on earlobe
and nape – shoots himself

in the crotch.
The Lady of Sorrows
glows in her niche.

King's Paramour

I scour the meadows for rue; dam the place
where he'll come with a compress of willow and juniper,
feverfew, white hellebore.

When he withdraws, I leap out of bed,
drink a flagon of sweet basil tea; burn over
hot coals the hoof of a mule;

swallow dittany, caper-spurge, marjoram, iris;
sit still, watch the moon. If needs be, I provoke
the red gush with mandrake and scammony,

colocynth, lavender, gentian and thyme.
If I grow big, I draw out the fruit
of my womb (as I must) with a poultice

of acorns and irises, burdock and dill.
Still, whether the Queen remain barren
or no, next year I'll bear him

a son; catch a hare, kill a pig. But tonight
(cross my heart, swear to die) I will smear my dark lips
with sisymbrium, cyclamen, unicorn dung.

Let him come.

Les Grands Seigneurs

Men were my buttresses, my castellated towers,
the bowers where I took my rest. The best and worst
of times were men: the peacocks and the cockatoos,
the nightingales, the strutting pink flamingos.

Men were my dolphins, my performing seals; my sailing-ships,
the ballast in my hold. They were the rocking-horses
prancing down the promenade, the bandstand
where the music played. My hurdy-gurdy monkey-men.

I was their queen. I sat enthroned before them,
out of reach. We played at courtly love:
the troubadour, the damsel and the peach.

But after I was wedded, bedded, I became
(yes, overnight) a toy, a plaything, little woman,
wife, a bit of fluff. My husband clicked
his fingers, called my bluff.

Props for the Parting Scene

I catch the last train. Hang from the strap.

You stay hunched on the receding platform
like a spy: a beard glued to your chin,

eyes behind shades, a newspaper you feign interest in,
as I hurtle down the track;

watch you grow small.

Ventriloquist's Dummy

You lever my jaws, make your claptrap
shoot from my mouth. There's a stamping
of feet. Wolf-whistles. Catcalls.

I burn, turn my face from the crowd
when I feel your thumb press on my gusset,
your falsetto rise in my throat.

Offstage, I gag when you come
on the stump of my tongue. You project
not a sound through my lips till I action

my jaws, spit your codpiece back into
your lap. Then the roaring begins.
Between us we bring the house down.

Still Life with Balcony

In this photograph you are three.
You sit on a chair, frowning,
hiding your broken teeth.

You are wearing a hand-knit jersey
with your initials on the chest.
They say you did not cry

when you discovered papa dead.
You clung to mamma's skirts.
But up she leaped,

made for the balcony,
dragging you behind her,
fingers tangled in her pleats.

She billowed like a sail
as she plunged; your hand
clutched at thin air as you

smashed into the wrought-iron
rail. Uncle Pedro reeled you in
like a fish;

blood in your mouth.

Mad about José

Anna went mad when she met José.
She threw off her diamonds, glass slippers, mink coat.
She put on an apron. She scrubbed his floor.
Her knees swelled up like purple hearts.

One midnight he fell in the door, fumbling
with cufflinks and flies. Anna loosened his tie
and put him to bed. Undaunted by bristle
and reek, the rasp of his tongue, she asked

for a kiss. His fist on her backbone, he pushed himself
in. Knuckled down, cracked her sternum, came yelping,
his paws on her rump. Then collapsed in a coma,
his face to the wall. Anna licked herself down,

washed him off. On the cusp of each breast, bruises
like rainbows, blue, purple and black. She bent over
the sink. She pounded his handkerchief. Mangled
his Y-fronts. Gyrating around with the handle,

she just could not stop, till she thought of the knot
she would make in his tie as he slept. Funny
how quick he turned blue, purple, black. Anna dressed
in her diamonds, glass slippers, mink coat. Left her knees

and her apron. No note.

It happened in Parque Güell

In Parque Güell water gushes
from the mouths of salamanders;
minarets sparkle in the sun.

You took me thirty-six times
in my dress of lavender and pink,
my hem frothy at the knee.

He took me once; his head
in a black tent, his tripod
sizzling in the heat.

He threw my image in a bucket,
offered me a baby
while we waited.

The lace at the end of my dress
weighed me down. I merged
with the mosaics.

He gave me my picture
in a cardboard frame.
'You like?'

My hand shook
as I offered him silver
in exchange.

Postulant

The cloister hems the novice in;

the fountain laughs, the well is deep.
She cannot sleep. She wraps the wimple
round her head, her cheeks,
her chin and neck. Behind the iron
grille she hears his step.

For morning Mass he chooses her
to vest him in the chasuble
and alb. He calls her
'Friend in Christ' and puts the host
upon her tongue. She grips her beads

and guards her eyes. He beckons her
again to hold The Book,
to ring the bell, to pour the water,
fill the cup; to feed the incense-burner
with the olibanum, styrax

and the cascarilla bark.

I saved them in mid-winter

I saved them in mid-winter.
Sat a boiling kettle on the ice
to melt a ring of air
so they could breathe.

Mint, weed and stone. Black water.

It could have been a cat.
Some say a heron got them
or that they died of fright
when crazed, in her first heat,
my bitch jumped in the pond.

Mint, weed and stone. Black water.

The fish just disappeared.
The staring palm-tree knows;
the honeysuckle, ivy plant,
geranium, hydrangea.

Mint, weed and stone. Black water.

I was quite fond of one:
a hunch-backed carp. He used to raise
his head above the murk
to get a pet; his rounded fish-mouth
open for a kiss.

Mint, weed and stone. Black water.

[53]

Burial

I made a little coffin
for my womb,
of hardwood, lined with velveteen
and plush.

I went to my own funeral,
behind the garden
shed; summoned angels
to escort me

into Paradise. The honeysuckle
wept.
The purple fuchsia bled
upon the ground.

I rang the blue-bells loud.
And in the hush
I cut the sod and sank the box
and topped it

with a stone. Lilies sprouted
in the grass:
Amaranthus, Agapanthus,
Amaryllis.

Snapdragons guard the spot.

The Photograph

The photograph
on your memorial card
is darker than the original,

smudged – a carbon copy.

Someone's black thumbprints
have been all over your face:
you're hard to see, getting

fainter all the time.

Passage

The teased-up earth
settles.
Nettles sting
in the ducts.

We buried you
today.
Firmed you
in.

The grass seed is
down.
The water
poured.

There is a stir
among the stars:

a cosmic shift;
a making way.

Earthing

The vet gave her back to me
in a jar eight inches tall,
so heavy, my heart sank
under the weight.

When I poured her into the earth,
a blur of fur and bone
slipped through my fingers
like silk.

By August, the lid of her grave
was lush again,
marked only by distance
from flagstone and shrub.

I measure her whereabouts now
in the span of my hands
over grass, track her in the sands
of time.

Playing the Bones

The bones I feel inside my skin
are scaffolding that holds me in.

Earth will glean them when I'm chaff,
and wafted off.

Those bones will be an implement,
an ornament or instrument.

Fingers will wrap themselves around
the hollow sound.

They'll play the bones *fortissimo*,
disturb me when I'm lying low.

Intent on resurrection – spring,
or some such thing.

Envelope of Skin

In an envelope of skin,
in a box of bone
I live. Jointed arms,
legs, fingers, toes,
ankles, elbows,
shoulders. The small
shovels of my collarbone.
The caterpillar of my
spine. The wide plates
of my hips.

In an envelope of skin,
in a box of bone
I live. Endless skeins
of hair push through
the epidermis. A hundred
years' supply of nail crouches
inside my fingertips
and under the cushions
of my toes.

Drums hide in the swirl
of my ear; a bridge
crosses my nose.

My belly a factory,
a recycling plant,
a compost heap.
My pelvis a girdle,
a breeding-ground,
a nursery.

The sponges of my lungs,
the pump of the heart,
the pulse at wrist
and neck
and temple.

Alone in my cave
I quest, striking matches
as I go. Paintings
in blood and excrement glow
on my palaeolithic walls.

Itineraries of Gold

Elephants, embroidered in silk,
circle the hem of my skirt.
On my upper arm, the bangles.
In the centre of my forehead,
the painted sign.
Around my neck, the gold.

Frowning, you walk beside me,
counting your profits
on an abacus of precious stones.
Until the sickle moon cuts
through the night sky,
you will not rest.

Then your brown fingers
will uncover the abacus
of my body: its taut wires,
its precious stones.

Outside our tent, elephants
will sink to their knees,
lean into the sand;
heavy in their garments
of ivory and leather.

Sweet Nothings

Your kisses were marshmallow
osculations on my lips,
in the lapse between the
conversation lozenges.

His were gelatinous confections,
rum and butter,
caramels.

Dark liqueurs, bilabial plosives,
glottal stops.
Honey-drops to suck

till cock-crow, when he gave me
fricatives.
Set

love-bites round my neck
like fudge; filled me
with Turkish Delight (Oh Hadji Bey!).

Left me
a jelly baby.

Postman's Knock

Your letters are like folded moons on onionskin,
suns pleated into envelopes, opaque Mallorcan
pearls.

You send me things: a diamond ring, a glass
of pink champagne, an antique fan, a high comb
for my hair.

You send me water from the Canaletes fountain;
ripe apricots at Christmas, marzipan
for January the Sixth.

The seasons come and go. You send me virgin snow
from Nuria, a piece of ancient rock
from Montserrat;

the songs of Lluís Llach. I lie in bed
all day at fever pitch and wait
for postman's knock.

The propositions that he pushes through the letterbox
(along with your dispatches) land
like homing-pigeons

in the hall; drive me insane
with their damn *cu-cu-ru-cu-cú.*

Chacun à son goût

I went to Chartres for windows; angled my neck
to the stained light.

You did your cathedral thing: merged
with the oak pew;

lowered your lids over eyes blue as the glass.

GETHSEMANE DAY

(2006)

Barbie

I made a doll of Plasticine
and spit; a witless,
empty-headed thing with shredded carrot
hair.

I dressed her in potato-skins
and wrapped a cobweb round her
like a cloak. I gave her
periwinkle shoes

and fishy feet. I soaked and mashed
the *Irish Times* in glue
and shaped a face, with rotten eggs
for eyes,

a furred banana nose,
and rows of rows of green fluorescent
teeth.

[Step-]Mother

'Mother' is a verb, said Joseph, not a noun.
And Joseph knows.

The 'step-' who mothered him, when mother (noun)
could not, poured love (another verb)
through the umbilicus of every day, non-stop,
to feed him and his siblings, and their father:
cord-bound forever to his severed brood.

Grief Therapy

Mastectomied Mavis was short a few tits; hunter
and gatherer, sharp in the wits, she savaged
the great hooded crows that invaded her patch, she gutted
the frogs in mid-leap; she challenged the foxes,
made mincemeat of voles, she skewered black rats on her teeth.

Her mate was a pacifist, gentle and neat, a small-boned
Mahatma with socks on his feet, the most
that he caught was a woodlouse, a worm or a leaf. Enslaved
by his passion for Mavis, his velcro-tongue stuck
to her coat, he wore himself out. The night that he gave up

the ghost, Mavis said: 'Shite! Now I'll have to attend
to myself.' But she could not perform her toilette.
Her fur lost its glitz. Sex with stray toms wasn't nice.
Listless, she lay on the shelf to consider
her plight. Mesmerized by the twitch in her tail, lopped it off

with one bite.

Queen's Ransom

A necklace of Venetian glass,
a brass bell from Tibet,
rough opals from a mine
in Mexico,

a fossil of a fish;
a bangle from Arabia,
a doll from Bogotá,
an elephant

with sapphire eyes, his cap embroidered
with a golden thread;
a gypsy's alphabet of beads,
a packet

of hibiscus seeds, an ocean
in a periwinkle shell;
an icon of St Nicholas,
a kopek

from a Russian prince, a diamond ring,
a samovar, the swirling curtain
of the Northern Lights;
an angel

on a pin, wings tangled up
with baubles in a biscuit tin
and Valentines in plastic bags,
tea-caddies

full of lies; the ashes
of a favourite cat, a baby tooth;
a clock of sand, a drop of blood
from Padre Pio's

hand; the invitations
never sent, the hair that I wore
ankle-length, a heart suspended
in formaldehyde.

How to see Wales

He gave me full instructions *re* weather,
season, light, cloud cover over the sea.
The sun at an angle like this (he showed me
his finger and thumb) and the sky just like that
(he tilted the brim of his hat).

Conditions being right (he assured me)
I would suddenly see the white place
where the chin of Wales dips in the sea
(not all its face at one go, nor its holy head).
But to make up for that, Snowdonia, a bit farther
back.

Happy Families

When I was six, with sucking fingers clamped
between my teeth, I rocked in bed and sang
myself to sleep; blew out the light for Dadda.

We counted sheep together; played Tip and Tig,
and Blind Man's Buff, O'Grady Says Do This,
Do That. I Spy. When I got tired, Dadda

took out his hand to shuffle and deal, shuffle
and deal. He made me split the deck; taught me
the Three-Card Trick, showed me the Joker.

Death by poisoning

Was it a hooded crow
that dropped the deadly meat
onto the lawn?

Or was it a cross-eyed cat
that left a rat half-eaten there
at dawn?

Or was it a madman,
standing at the gate,
who fed you poisoned bones
you gladly ate?

Were you a changeling
sent to us that day,
when fairies took
the real Bracken away?

The changeling's dead.
We left her in a sack
for fairies to reclaim,
bring our dog back.

She never came.
They left us grief-trees
wailing at the wall.
And that was all.

My heart lives in my chest

My heart lives in my
chest. I know it's there.
But now the rogue will often
disappear, and leave me
stranded in my scarecrow
mind. It's so unkind.
What did I do to make her run
away? – I ask myself each
day. What did I do,
or what did I do not
or just in part, to make my
heart pack up and run
away?

The house inside my chest is
empty now – a vacant lot;
the weeds grow wild in there,
and still heart not come back.
Soon the foundations will be swept
away, and underneath the chest's vast
empty skies, only the cries that
echo from afar, of some strange
flapping bird, no longer navigating by a
star.

Trophy

The bull sinks to its knees; the dagger
plunged to the hilt in its scabbard
of flesh. The trumpets blare out.
Men bite their cigars, throw their hats
in the air. The women crack open
their fans; kick up polka-dot skirts.

They tear at their bosoms with red sharpened
nails; fling suspenders and brassières
into the ring, their telephone
numbers attached to the stems of
roses, carnations, camellias, begonias.

The matador smirks in his costume
of lights. Takes a bow. Blows back kisses.
He lops off the ears of the bull,
the black globes of its testicles. Looking
around, sees my whitening face,
throws the whole bloody lot in my lap.

Curette

Down in Dun Laoghaire
the vets are at work,
pale green gowns over their usual tweed.

She's in pup. Mongrel-mounted.
A pedigree bitch,
like myself. But the bloodline's secure.

This time they won't scour
the womb
with the spoon-shaped curette.

They will fix her for good.
Like myself.
No more dogs at our gate.

Ménage à trois

I wear my mother on my back
till I am twenty-one;
her rope and tackle anchored
to my omphalos.

When I meet you, I tidy up
my act. Place my mother
with her snorkel in a sack.
At thirty-five,

half-smothered in hibiscus nights,
I lie upon the Caribbean
shore, my mother
like a bolster

in the sand between myself
and you. I buckle
when your humming-bird is inches
from my skirt.

I drag my mother up the aisle
to help me say: 'I do'.
Beneath her Greta Garbo hat,
her camouflage

of lace, confetti-ed out,
she turns her sideways face to you
and begs for secateurs
and pruning-shears,

a sword with cutting edge.
I clutch my blanket, suck my thumb,
pull at the pulsing vein
and rein her in.

I bring her home to share the marriage
bed. Her eyes behind
their cataracts, she doesn't see you
come

with pickaxe, hatchet, slashers
from the shed to cut the cord.
I birth a wrinkled baby
on a string.

I haemorrhage and spurt.
You make a tourniquet
out of your shirt.

Four Haiku

Sunlight in gutter,
butterbright, apricot, peach,
October, leaf-thief.

*

In the tall windows
of their eyes, cats crouch, under
pelmets of warm fur.

*

Cats knead on my knees,
pumping paws, piercing claws, I
bleed. Oh, but the purrs.

*

Purple hearts sprouting
unseen in the forests of
winter broccoli.

Bones

I feel the bones that will lie in my grave;
They have for me a close familiarity;
They live inside me, snug, in their enclave.

The bones that were fine webs when in the cave
Of mother's womb, all hidden in obscurity,
I feel the bones that will lie in my grave.

My scaffolding, the bones; the ringing concave
Vault that holds my brain's irregularity;
They live inside me, snug, in their enclave.

When finally I'm winnowed, earth will save
The bones alone, prove their superiority.
I feel the bones that will lie in my grave.

The bones will lose their marrow, but they're brave –
They'll hollow themselves out for more sonority;
They live inside me, snug, in their enclave.

When I turn round, Lot's wife, for one last wave,
The bones will wave back with a dry hilarity.
I feel the bones that will lie in my grave;
They live inside me, snug, in their enclave.

'If I should wake before I die'

If I should wake before I die,
I'll take that beam out of my eye,
I'll sail a boat, I'll learn to fly,
I'll make a spongy apple pie.

Philomena McGillicuddy becomes unstuck

When he was big and strong and hairy,
she was like the Virgin Mary;
schoolboys masturbated nightly,
the Pope in Rome was God Almighty:
fear was the glue.

Now he's small and weak and balding,
she's got the hots, in fact she's scalding;
schoolboys booze and come home bleary,
the Pope in Rome is airy-fairy:
the world's undone.

Money is a piece of plastic,
sin is gone, it's all elastic;
Philomena's hesitating,
no, by God, she's masturbating:
fear was the glue.

Dream

Mittens on your breasts: those shrines where tossing hands,
cold as bottles, rattle pectorals in pockets of loose skin.

Your body hair wound round me like a scarf, I nest,
a winter bird; and beg the duvet's benediction on cold feet.

The cradle rocks. The knitting-needles click. Toes press
upon the pedalos: the tides of feet that push me out to sea.

The hips of winter, wide as a cathedral, stand firm
in my back yard. The wind roars in my ears. Gothic ships

like mating cats whip up the ocean. Swans like driven snow
stand frozen on the ice. The baldy nuns come clacking

yellow lips. Their veils are plastic bags. Lovers lie
in separate beds; reach out stone hands and touch across
    the great divide.

I rip the rosaries from the sweaty sheets; the Finnish mattress
ripples at my sleeve; the litanies drone on,

stillborn as a sodality, infertile as a Child of Mary,
I wear the wide blue ribbon; hang around my neck

the millstone medal. The indoor shoes of dream
caress my head like a school beret. *Cruci dum spiro fido.*

And once again I'm huddled in my childhood coat, red velvet,
tightly belted at the waist, and bow before the sanctuary lamp.

Ancestors

Radiant each time we come,
she pulls her ancestors out,
and warms them
with her tongue.

They glow with her life.
She explains the links,
gives us
the low down.

But her husband plays dumb,
wrings his hands on his lap,
tweed knees
slack.

Paulo Freire's theory revisited

Confined with her mate in the cattery, she
belted him one on the chin;
ate from his plate;
he grew thin.

Back home in their usual place,
it was all hit and miss;
sometimes she allowed him to kiss her,
to stick his tongue into her ear,
rasp at her neck, lick her face;
then, to show who was boss,
she slapped him, for nothing, again.

Neutered and past it, it wasn't for
sex she invited him into her bed,
but for animal heat;
when he'd warmed up her feet,
she gave him a sock on the jaw,
hooshed him out with a tortoiseshell paw.

Muling, he skulked round the house,
shat on the furniture, spewed in his dish,
mass-murdered his catnip-filled toys,
except for Milupa, his favourite mouse;
he took her apart, called her a fart,
randy cow, filthy slut, friggin' bitch,
wished himself dead when he ate out her heart;

it was small as a jelly-bean,
sweeter than saccharine,
heavy as lead.

I spend the night

I spend the night with the cathedral; cool
my fevered body on the stone.
Stretched out along its length, I listen to the inward
hesitation of its bells, the angel voices
rising from the choir behind the screen;
the organ-music pumping through my bones.

Crowning Glory

When the boy who has the magic
ran his fingers through your hair,
you lost your sullen looks;
loosed your locks.
Bold as brass.

You blew up like a balloon;
shed your gymslip, your school tie
and the medal auntie brought you
back from Lourdes.
Bold as brass.

Your parents fired a shot
across your bows; but you sailed on,
a tall ship with a treasure
in your hold.
Bold as brass.

The boy with the magic
assisted at the birth.
Your mother paced outside,
beside herself.
Bold as brass.

You placed the little baby
in a decorated basket.
Your hair cascaded round her
like the rain.
Bold as brass.

The boy who has the magic
comes each night to brush your hair.
Sparks fly in the offended rooms
below.
Bold as brass.

You skip out to paint the town,
strap the baby to your breast,
and let the bell-ropes of your hair
dingle-dangle.
Bold as brass.

You trap your mop in plaits.
You twist it into rings.
You wind it in a chignon
or a bun.
Bold as brass.

You pick it up and wave it.
You iron it till it's flat.
You hide it in a kerchief
or a hat.
Bold as brass.

But you never bleach or dye it,
never clip it, trim or cut it.
You just buff and shine
the top-knot on your crown.
Bold as brass.

Between my upper thighs

Between my upper thighs, the bivalve seethes.
I sit for hours in the white and narrow bath.
I must needs have my ablutions. Kitchen salt in the
solution. With hands flapping, water lapping and
silver benedictions from the taps.

Sobs rack my chest

Sobs rack my chest like uncontrollable
laughter, making a knocking
sound. They're gone and I'm stranded.
My compass is lost in the sand. I have
been crawling on my hands and knees
for days. My glasses are salted over and
cracked. The horizon has merged with the
sky. There is no edge from which to hang
my plumb-line. No ledge on which to lay
my spirit-level. And you are outside piling logs,
working on your own wreckage.

Live Model

In the slant of the loft
I take off my clothes.
You half-close your eyes,
size me up, lay me down
on a canvas. You scratch
at your beard, you colour me
in, glaze me over.

Under the curve
of my belly, I notice
a stipple of hog's hair,
a slash of magenta,
a mish-mash of gesso
and ink. You gaze
at your unfinished work.

So I dress, slip the latch,
make my way down
the stairs. At the click
of stiletto on marble,
the concierge peers
out the hatch, follows me
with his nicotine eyes.

Pedicure

They bound my soft-boned feet. Folded the neat toes
under. Laced my shoes tight.

My lover found me tethered to my gait.
He did his best with pumice-stone and razor-blade,

mercurochrome, lint. He gave me a charm
bracelet. Lent me his arm. My toes unfurled

like wings, spread out like flippers. Nothing can
contain me now, but these vast velcroed slippers.

Ghost Train

I pay sixpence to go round the loop. Slide the coin
with the greyhound and harp from my red pillar-box.
Slip it into the hand of the garlicky carnival-man.

He whispers, as always: 'That's grand'. But this time
his face is too close to my cheek. There's a shag
of thick hair on his chest. He half-jests in my ear: 'Not a
    word

to your folks and the next ride's on me.' He follows
my spark as I clickety-clack round the track.
Skeletons hang in the dark, lighting up, as we pass.

I pretend he's a friendly old dog when he jumps in
beside me and rests his white head on my knee.
But I find I can't slap him away when he opens his flippety

-flap, takes the blanket-pin out of my pleats, leaves a
slobber all over my lap.

Last night the itch

Last night the itch was a witch
poking her switch in there.
The twitch of the sphincter no salt
or balm could repair. Aware not to
touch, I lie, awake,
as night sizzles through the garden.

A broomstick, if I may. A hot poker.
Something flowery and cool. Something smooth
as the calamine pink of the lilies
that cup in my pond. As the calm green
pads that float on the moon-slabbed
water.

Wild strawberries I picked for him,
fairy berries; a crop;
I filled a whole thimble, right to the
top. A silver container,
cool; embossed.

I rave between blue sheets, my body
aflame. I crave snowy peaks;
a wedge of ice tucked in my
buttocks.

Deansgrange

Please to remember, please to remember, Beth
in her shroud of cut stone. Mary wrapped in her blanket of
    mud.
Uncle John in his great bed of weeds, calling out as I pass:
please to remember.

Eliza, who died on the ship sailing home from the Gulf,
and the husband who pined till he joined her, lying on top.
And storeyed above them their water-logged daughter,
    Miranda,
who threw herself in. *Please to remember. Please.*

Dora, who's trapped in the roots of an oak-tree. Janet,
weighed down under pink marble chips. Marjorie, beads
round her fingers, a crucifix nailed to her chest. And Alex,

who flew his own plane round the world, now parked in
    the hangar
of death. *Please to remember.* Angels who freeze
on their plinths as they wait for the Kingdom to come;
    Jacob's ladder
slung down from the sun. *Please to remember. Please.*

S.O.S.

I tied her to a chair
and put her in the care
of John of God.

They locked her in a box
of glass and stone:
a home from home.

Her skirt sagged at the hem.
She drummed upon her knee
and thought of me.

I never heard her gentle tap
upon my heart
when she slipped out.

I never heard her softly wrap
the sea around her
like a shroud.

My life was just too loud.

Crazy for another baby

María places the china doll
in the middle of the bed,
lights three candles as the elders
bid her do.

She plies the doll with kisses,
turns the key stuck in its back.
Fingers clenched and eyelids batting,
it cries: 'Mamma'.

María rocks the doll,
its china face pressed to her breast.
She begs Jesus and His Mother
to have pity.

Juan Manuel, María's son,
a boy of twelve, lies fast asleep.
He is summoned in a dream
to go to Mamma.

As he glides into her room
a good six inches off the floor,
María swears it's her dead husband,
Juan Ramón.

She thanks Jesus and His Mother,
nods her head, blows out the candles,
bids the boy lie down beside her,
sucks him in.

Fingers clenched and eyelids batting,
Juan Manuel shakes off his Mamma,
wafts away, a good six inches
from the floor.

María stretches out her hand,
sets a taper to the wick,
lights three candles as the elders
bid her do.

Harlequined

Harlequined in his dressing-gown, I sleep.
My arms, lozenges of yellow
and blue, lying under the sheets,
shake themselves loose. My dog,
dreaming at the foot of the stairs,
emits muffled woofs; her paws,
flashing like unicorn hoofs,
knocking sparks off the sky. I turn over,
take off through the roof.

Gethsemane Day

They've taken my liver down to the lab,
left the rest of me here on the bed;
the blood I am sweating rubs off on the sheet,
but I'm still holding on to my head.

What cocktail is Daddy preparing for me?
What ferments in pathology's sink?
Tonight they will tell me, will proffer the cup,
and, like it or not, I must drink.

My daddy's a skeleton

My daddy's a skeleton under the ground
in the grave where there's room for more;
I wonder will Sister Death telephone first
or just barge in at the door
when she comes for me in her black limousine
with her black dog at her heels,
and will I have time to pack my bags
before the death-knell peals?
Will I be like Marie who swam for two hours
on the day she was taken away,
or more like Janet who had a few months
to get ready and have her say?
Will I be like Laura who went for a nap
at home, and never woke up,
or Rosie who lingered for over a year
while sipping the fatal cup?
Will I ever be ready, I muse today,
as I lie in my cosy bed,
will I always be needing a little more time
to get things straight in my head?

Fruits of the Womb

The intervention
along the bikini-line
yielded fibroids
big as melons.

Total weight
(appendages
included)
nine pounds nine.

Freed Spirit

I am swallowed, feet first, by the scanning machine
until only a wisp of my hair remains
to be seen.

Strapped down by the hips, I'm immobile except for
my lips. Blanketed up to the chin,
I pretend

I am taking a nap. But the plugs in my ears are like
crap when the elephant trumpets begin.
Jack Rabbit

is thumping a hole in my skull. There's a lunatic
trying to get in. Birds of prey swoop down
and peck.

Niagara cascades down my neck. Doctors,
oblivious, stare at their flickering screens.
My image

jumps up, a glow emanating from pelvis and
abdomen, thorax and fingers and toes.
Can they see

how I'm gyred through the ether and reach for the stars?
Can they see in this stalk of wild fennel, the twinkle
and spark?

Aeons pass by in a ticking of nuclear
clocks till a voice on the intercom crackles
and pops:

'Remember the bell you can squeeze if the going gets
rough.' 'Much obliged,' I reply, in a wheeze that
comes out of

the grave. I force my eyes through to the back of my
head, half-see them as darkly they wave.

Dark and furry as the night

Dark and furry as the night,
he made himself thin,
squeezed through death's railing
without a sigh,
trailing his broken tail.

I am like a great white whale
still stranded here
on my ebbed beach,
my killer teeth gleaming
in the moonlight,
a red gash in my side.

Sea creatures with webbed feet
and ductless eyes
try to turn back the tide.

Radiotherapy

Nurses feed the nuclear machine that hovers
overhead with lumps of lead.

Vast areas of me are thus protected from the beams,
or so it seems. Between each session

Kathleen and Olivia, Aileen, May and Margaret
take turns to push my pelvis round

about, ensuring that the rays will hit their target.
The side-effects are as expected,

but for one: my pubic hairs fall out.

Bedlam

This Christmas no star.
A trail of prescriptions leads to the cancer ward;
she lies on a mattress of straw,
the animal breath at her neck.

Nurses with antlers set canulas
into her veins, tinsel her blood
through the drip.
Camels unfurl their black lips,
eat her hair with their fluorescent teeth.

Adeste, adeste; St Nicholas
brings her a bell, to ting-a-ling,
ting-a-ling, ting-a-ling, ting
till she's well.

The dream-world of my pillow

Things float in the dream-world of my pillow
as I wrap my arms round the billowing sheets
of wind. But the storm escapes me,
rocking the ship of the house, the dry waves
bashing against the bricks and the glass
eyes and smoky funnels of home.
I hear the men shouting; sailors on the ropes and masts
and the wind sluicing through the
trees. The sun flashes on the polished wooden
decks and in the silver mirrors as the men
rattle their tools. They ring like bells across the wavy
lawns, while clouds fluff past, fast, on smooth
sky-tracks, invisible to the eye. And now the
hammer is thudding, and there is scraping
and the sound of wood bumping on wood.
Hollow sounds, rich sounds. Drums in the
garden. And Andrew is below deck, looking for
solutions, as I sit on my bunk or sway in my
hammock, watching my shadow on the ceiling.

I swap the Mediterranean

I swap the Mediterranean for a gleaming white
bath, sand-coloured carpets,
Valencian tiles and a wide-swinging window of
    glass.

I swap turquoise waves for a bubble of
soap, a cupful of salt,
a silvery tap.

I am the sacrifice at the new
Mass. I lie on a plain sheet of
paper; a head-rest of sponge.
They offer me up on an altar of
tin.

Instead of the tinkling of bells, or the
clappers of wood – for the season is
Lent – I hear the low beeps of the
radiotherapy machine. Its great arm
entwines me; its deep-socketed eye
beams at me.

Half-naked, my pelvis exposed,
my hands out of the way, criss-crossed on my
chest, I endure; stare through closed
lids at nothing on earth.

Life Boat

I made an ark out of my skull, an upturned hull with no mast, sail
or rigging,
except the switch of hair that still grew wild, as when I was
a child,
around the everlasting fontanelle.

I blocked the holes, I brushed the curving bone with bitumen
and pitch.
Safe from the world, I hid there all alone, till suddenly
dark stirrings
of my mind released the beasts within:

the onocentaur, oversexed, came rushing in; the manticora
grinding
all its teeth; the bonnacon with flaming bum; the fierce
monocerous;
the crocodile, the savage spotted pard;

the great baboon; the parandrus, the asp, the flying jaculus,
the seps.
At loggerheads, we drifted towards Armenia atop
the rising flood
and teetered on the pinnacles of Ararat.

For forty days or weeks or months or years, I waited
for the waters
to subside. The creatures in my cranium increased
and multiplied.
I said my prayers. I cried. The might of heaven

pounded on my roof. At last, the muddy hydrus
(the only serpent
on the side of angels) led me out. And lo, God's gifts
lay scattered
all about: rare Paracletes with tongues of fire;

an Englishman with ropes and gamp; a singing bird, an olive
    branch,
a box of nard,
a spirit-lamp, safe passage to the cedar-groves of Lebanon.

Mid-Winter

Cut flowers in a vase this night,
orange, golden and snow-white;
dark green leaves and darker stems,
take me where the dark earth bends
its darkened forehead to the east,
where Lucy lights the candles for her feast.

LONG-DISTANCE SWIMMER

(2009)

Mother's kitchen

Mother's kitchen – it's laid out
on the terrazzo floor;
marble galaxies beneath her feet,

dead wasps in the jam-jar;
the Aga throbs with heat.
And Maggie,

        her bag
full of stolen trinkets, humdy-dumdies
down the stairs, her hair sticking out,

out like a bottle-brush,
her sister still threatening

to throw herself off
the end of
the pier.

Death by drowning

You pin your hair up in a bun,
step out of your skirt, dive in.
The sea shivers round your waist
like a petticoat of silk.

You swim past pretty cottages
and rows of boats fragmenting
in the waves. Outside the harbour
the undertow twirls you about.

You turn on your back; head
for the island through buffet and toss.
Cross-currents tear at your grips,
pull down your hair. Blinded,

you kick at the sea. Arms windmill and
grope. Water spills into your
mouth, sandbags you down
through piston-rod, hammer and pound.

For an instant, the heap of your hair
floats like a raft on the spot
where the sea sucks you in. Half-daft,
too late to beg pardon,

we wait for your wreckage to land.
We harden our grief into rituals,
requiems, wreaths. You drift back
in your own sweet time.

Going your own way

You swim out in your underwear,
your skirt discarded
on the harbour wall.

You don a mantilla of spume,
the rope of your hair trailing
like kelp in your wake.

You head for the Kish. Its bright eye
blinking a way forward
like a sanctuary lamp.

You crawl over seas of granite.
Flurries of foam pull
at your petrified ankles.

You hear water-bells clang;
clappers of iron and salt
salute you *en passant*.

You lean on waves of cold
comfort before
going
                              down

Fledgling

Cooped up in a birdcage at eighty,
she pecks on a cuttlefish bone,
decks out her new home: silver bells,
ladders and swings.

In mirrors that dangle like moons
from the sky, she finds look-alike friends:
discreet parakeets with scimitar
beaks like her own.

But they're dumb. She tempts them with rum
from Jamaica, with sips of the sweetest
Jerez, with truffles and chocolates,
with pink gin and cakes.

She gives them a peek at her treasures,
gold sovereigns, carbuncles and rings;
the knick-knacks he gave her, the way
he enslaved her, the rubies

he slung round her neck. What the heck.
She kohls her frail eyelids, blushes
her cheeks, hangs upside-down
on her perch. She ruffles

her feathers, she whistles and sings;
she feels the first stretch

of her wings.

Chez moi

I'm only at home on the hill now,
walking my dog among trees,
or curled out the back with my cat.

People – I take them or leave them;
it's all touch and go, except
for the man in the deer-stalker hat

who pops up now and then in my bed.
Shadowy children flit round
in the wings. I used to be yearning

but now I've no time for such things.
I light scented candles. I stand
on my head. I make no more scenes.

Parents die off or wear thin, but drag on.
Siblings of sixty and more
are bickering still. It's a scream.

We're all too far gone. I've named
my executor, drawn up my will;
I can feel my hide thicken. Inside

there's new skin. I can't hang around people
for ever, I've got things to do
on the moon. Trees leave me alone,

don't ask questions, are there;
candelabra of seasons in bud,
fairy lights that switch on in the gorse.

There's a door in the rock
at a place where the salt sea flows
into the sky; I can squeeze through
to Wales.

The see-saw

Lurching on the see-saw of marriage,
the hard plank under your bottom,
you gasp at the repeated jolts
that shiver your timbers.

You grasp at straws, your wedding dress
coming away in your hands.
Your teeth are bared,
your eyes squeezed tight.
You are losing your
balance.
The black mop of your hair
flops over your face,
and your veil is wild
around your ears.

The third finger of your left hand
is branded with a ring.
As the lurching continues,
you struggle to pull your skirt
down over your knees.
One of your shoes has fallen
into the mud.

Your mother can't help you now.
She sits at right angles to you,
heavy in her apron, staring
at her lap.

A little girl stands with her back
to the wall, sucking her thumb.
She waits for her turn. She has a butterfly
bow in her hair and white wedding
shoes on her feet.

Forbidden fruit

I

He loved dark chocolate, speckled melons, quince.
With fingers that were trembling, touched the ripening
fruits. His mother had to hide the sweet
preserves. He rooted round the attic till
he found the deep glass jars, and speared with knitting
needles woozy cherries, apricots
and peaches, drunken blue-black grapes.

A prince among his siblings (his mother said
that he could sing before he learnt to speak),
his parents, forty cousins, uncles, aunts,
the cooks and maids, the workers on the land,
all jumped at his command. They knew that
Federico, from the moment of his birth,
could hear the bells that ring beneath the earth.

A phosphorescent child (since lightning left its
kiss upon his cheek) he walked along
the river-paths, half-dazed among the willows
and the hollyhocks, wild celery and yellow-flowered
fennel, umbelliferous. He built an altar
on the garden wall, said Mass in mother's
frock; but when a troupe of puppeteers

arrived in town, he could not eat or sleep until
he'd torn the altar down, set up a little
theatre instead. He begged his old

wet-nurse to fashion rag and cardboard dolls.
And then he started on his puppet-plays.

2

In formal suit and white starched shirt and patent leather
shoes, he set out for the 'Resi'
in Madrid, his hair combed back to show his widow's
peak. Unspeakable the things he felt for
Salvador, Emilio. Their merest glances
left him flushed and weak.

3

Terrified of sex and sin, the swelling purple
aubergine, he crossed the ocean, paced Manhattan
streets. If only he could be a child
again and fall asleep on Cobos Rueda's
knee, and talk to plants and listen
to the stars. In waking dreams his favourite cousins
loomed: Aurelia (the one who hated

thunderstorms), Matilda and Clothilde.
The irrigation streams, the *regadío*,
kept flowing in his brain. Insane the winter
smell of pent-up water that came from every
house, the ghostly glow of oil-lamps newly

lit, the half-scorched wings of moths.
He used to be a *monaguillo* once,

an altar-boy, the Baby Jesus blessing him
with fingerless white hands. But now male lovers
beckoned him. He posed, Christ-like, against a tree,
his arms stretched out. And then succumbed. Delirious,
half-numbed, he wrote of nightingales and daggers;
of lemons, blood-red poppies, seedless fruits.

4

A lecture tour in Cuba set him free.
He swam with naked blackmen in the sea.
The sky was Málaga-blue and oh, the heat;
the endless beat of bongo-drums, the slow sad
habaneras, the rattle of a thousand beads
in hollow dried-out gourds. Drunk on the scent
of orchids and magnolias, and heady draughts of

sticky sugar-cane, he lost count of the
one-night stands, drew sustenance, they say,
from rum and cups of coffee, *champola de
guanábana* and pungent fat cigars.
Stretched on his bed in Hotel La Unión,
he read his poems to dozens of young men
and breakfasted on honey-bread at noon.

5

After a season in the Cuban sun,
Federico yearned again for Algeciras,
Cádiz, Alcalá de los Gazules,
and burned a trail for Spain. Granada was still
there; the Alpujarras, Cáñar,
La Calahorra and Guadix; the washerwomen
singing as before, the shepherds

with grave faces tending sheep, la Casa
del Zagal. The Virgin of Good Love
in her tin crown lit up her spangles, and Federico,
laughing, struck the window-bars of home
with a small metallic spoon and played
a wild carillon to the moon.

6

In August nineteen thirty-six, the death-squad came.
They trampled down the jasmine and the bright blooms
of the pomegranate bushes; primed their rifles,
roaring out his name.

One Easter

One Easter you left me there
to walk the dry hills alone,
flies nesting in my hair,
the sun burning a hole
in my nape.

I walked past mountainy cows
with wooden bells and tongue-tied
Spanish shepherds tending
their sheep.

Up on the peak the Snow Virgin
did as she was bid. She heard your prayer.
She was there when the waterfall
leapt to its death; and was swept over
the black rocks below in a ragged white
drift.

She was there when I navigated
the swish-car roads, the hairpin bends,
the merry-go-round loops of the path
that led to your door. She was there
when your mother leaned out over the balcony
to soothe her tattered nerves
with the sound of water sucked
into hollow spaces, swirling like
a mad whippers in the gorges
waiting in the drowning-holes
for such as I,

left to walk the dry hills alone,
the flies nesting in my hair,
the sun burning a hole
in my nape. I wrapped my cardigan
round my head like a scarf
and reached, as I said, your mother's door.

She stared at me. Mute.
So I sang her a song in my own tongue.
Told her how far I had come
and how cruel was her son
who had cruelly left her
and me to walk the dry hills
alone.

She sat in a kitchen chair,
hands folded on her lap. We cried
and listened to the water suck. After,
she made me an omelette,
gave me some cooked ham still
wrapped in a bag, and rubbed ripe
tomatoes into a loaf of bread.
We ate. Drank the weak table wine.
Pale pink with a flush of sugar-water.
She called me her daughter.

Next morning, I picked myself up,
dragged myself to the station. Lost sight
of the Snow Virgin when the train swept me

away. Sparks jumped off the tracks when
we reached the next valley. But I did not
give up my devotion to her. Spurred on
by the fact that you left me to walk

the dry hills by myself. Till I found
your mother wandering there too.
We protected each other from the flies.
From the heat of the sun.

Christmas in the Pyrenees

Smells of hot chocolate and snow drift into the room.
With fingers on fire, I rush to the frozen pane.
I melt a peep-hole and look: the mountains rise sheer
like fat wax candles pressing against the sky.

Your mother is setting the table; she pokes at the stove.
She looks up at you with the usual sobs in her eyes.
Your stepfather rustles the paper; he works at his sums
with the butt of a pencil, moving his lips as he tots.

Cheap chandeliers hang low over our heads.
Your mother brings in the cups, lays her hand on your arm.
She sits in her chair, then straightens her apron and sighs.
The river flows down the ravine and past the back door.

It's Christmas and Jesus is laid on his bed of fake fur.
A halo held firm with two nails at the back of his neck.
His plaster legs beat at the air, his hands clasp in prayer.
His vitreous eyes, dark as hers, catching mine, catching yours.

Down in the village the Wise Men appear on a cart:
Balthazar, Melchior, Caspar, one daubed with soot.
Startling in scarlet and gold, their crowns at a tilt,
they trundle ahead of the crowd, throwing out sweets.

The small mountain ponies are panting, they strain at the slope;
steam swirls from their nostrils, sparks fly from their
    clattering hooves.
They come to a halt at the church; Mass-bells echo on rock
as we rise from the table in silence and glance at the clock.

Carlitos González Martínez makes
a desperate bid for freedom

His three-year-old face was an ivory moon.
He never got out:
the overweight toddler from Tamarit Street,
puffing great baby with infantile feet;
I led him away to the sea.

His three-year-old face was yoghurt and milk.
His little heart beat
like a drum in my fist when he took his first steps
from Tamarit Street. Not a minute too soon
I led him away to the sea.

I showed him the birds on the Ramblas, in cages,
the budgies and cockatoos,
parrots, canaries; the bare-bottomed monkeys
on silver-chain leashes, that screeched as Carlitos
passed by on his way to the sea.

We went to the market, bought apricots, peaches,
black olives and anchovies,
almonds and quinces; *chorizos, serranos,*
manchegos and *churros* to keep up our strength
as we came within sight of the sea.

We boarded the three-masted *Santa María,*
we chugged round the port
on the white *golondrina.* We sat on the beach
at the Barceloneta where oysters and octopus
dance in the diamond-bright sea.

We took the quick lift up Columbus's monument.
Paid a peseta
to peep through the telescope, scan the horizon
for new worlds and islands, Mallorca, Menorca,
not Tamarit Street where they never

heard tell of the sea. I went down by the stairs.
'But not I', cried Carlitos
González Martínez. An outgrown *putto*
with pink pudgy wings, he took to the air.
His three-year-old face a lit candle,

a rose, he waved *adiós* to Tamarit
Street and said 'Hello sea'
to the sea.

Gypsy dancer in the caves at Sacromonte

At first his castanets produced a fluttering,
a kind of small talk, sotto voce stuff.

And then there was a flurry in the brown cups
of his hands: a sound of birds all twittering

and bickering and cracking nuts. Trapped between
his palms, he held them on the very edge

of flight. With slow tap-tapping toes,
he moved along the full length of the cave

to where I stood, and there he stopped. I gulped the wine.
Suddenly,

his hands commotioning behind his back,
he teetered on his heels, his ankles

undulating, if you please, as though they'd turned
to butter, like my knees.

Waiting for Julio

Maria nearly died

when Julio came upon her, feeding slops to the pigs.
But it was love at first sight.

He made friends with her father, put a ring on her finger
and gave her a son.

In his letters from the Front, he called her 'My Jewel';
sent kisses to the boy.

While the Civil War raged, she slept on one half
of the bed, molly-coddled

the baby, kept Julio's pillows plumped up,
embroidered his name

in the linen, and busied herself with the sheets.
She soaked them in troughs

of dark water behind the house. She scrubbed them
on washboards of stone.

She dragged them up steps to the kitchen, in buckets
and basins and tubs.

She strung them out neat on a line that stretched taut
from her window to peaks

that poked holes in the sky. She pegged them on tight.
Clouds of carbolic

hung over the house and got under her skin.
All the other men died

in the war, or came back to the village, but Julio
hovered betwixt.

He appeared one day with a rug round his shoulders,
his eyes out on sticks.

He pushed past 'My Jewel', the baby, the bed,
and curled up in the cot;

plugging his ears with his whimpering hands,
he made soft sucking sounds

with his lips.

Back patio

Under the giant palm tree
behind the patio wall,
I suffer when I see the clay:
the place where tom cats shit
and slugs lay slime, and fronds
fall dead.

I stand on all four feet
and lock my joints. Project
my fur-balls onto broccoli
and honeysuckle, pink
and blue hydrangea.

The lily-cups sit on the water-table:
purple, pink and white.
The lily pads are green and flat.
Like plates.

I shoulder my three cats,
quick stroke and purr.
Inject the insulin.
Then back to work.
I clear away the excrement,
clean out the litter-tray,
the heaps of heavy sand,
dark perfume of testosterone,
the steroid-treated male.

Geraniums grow red and violent
in their tubs. Tomato vines
hang sweet. Sweet peas climb up
the bamboo pole and loop the loop.

Behind the giant palm
the tap is dripping.
The hose writhes like a snake.
It spits at spiders, lunges at the ants and aphids,
spouts at water-mint. It lashes
at the grey stone slabs, uproots
the tiny strawberries,
self-seeded in the gap.

Quadruped with my quadrupeds

Quadruped with my quadrupeds
I crawl. Cats under the arch
of my belly, tails erect, touch
the goddess of their plenty.

Yawning on summer walls
or stretching on the gravel,
I examine my claws, retracting
my nails when you pet me.

In my basket of cushions I wait
for your hand. Your fingerprints
carry my code. I embed
myself in the whorls
of your flesh.

All day, heavy as stone,
I rest on dark weaves
of desire, waiting
for you to come home.

Then you lift me, warm,
onto your shoulder,
and carry me down
to the shiny white door.

I tighten my claws
on your nape, nip
at your ear.

You prise me off gently,
unfurl me in the long grass.

Soon we are out of sight:
she-cat in season, howling,
receiving her mate.

Peregrino

Three sets of hands are upon him
as the needle probes for the vein
and plunges the purple of death
into the pain.

Rent with his cry, I stroke
the blind fur. 'It's alright', I lie.
He sinks on soft knees, falls
in a tangle of paws.

The nurse straightens his limbs,
lays him out on his side; his heart
like a bird in the dark flutter
of stethoscope.

Propped against walls that keep edging
away, I catch sight of his wide-open
eyes. His pupils dilate.
They wax like the moon,

fill the room
with a nocturnal
light.

Dog-kite

I used to hold her
by a silver chain
that linked us
like a vein.

Now she's a comet,
dammit,
all wag-tail
and bright eye.

I see her whizz
between the stars;
she flares and disappears
in the night sky.

She left her paw-marks
in the wet cement.

My fireworks, the stars

My fireworks, the stars
exploding over my head
tonight, whizzing around
clouds, regrouping in
dense clusters, scattering
again, fading, falling,
shooting, hiding behind the
chimneys, nesting in trees,
and resting, finally, in the glass
wells of my binoculars.

The stars explode over my
head. Dogs bark as they
crackle, sizzle, fizz and pop
across the sky. The three cats
leap into my lap, eyes big as
saucers, ears pointing backwards.
Claws hook, tails twitch.

My stars flare like matches
unsteady as sulphur flame
in the quiet nothingness of the
sky. I reach up and pick them
one by one like silver daisies
out of the black field over my head.
They glow and tinkle like bells.
They are quite prickly.
They burn as I string them round my neck.

At Winchester

We spend the night in the cathedral,
cool our fevered bodies
on the stone.

Stretched out along the full length
of the nave, ear to the ground,
we hear

the drowning waters lapping
in the crypt. Ravished angels
rhapsody

behind the screen. Somewhere between
the gargoyles and the carven
misericords,

recumbent figures sleep
as if they're dead. At break of day
we rise up

from our marble bed. Renew
our marriage vow. May Emily
and Swithin

help us now.

In December it's dark

In December it's dark
in Lapland.
You travel by sleigh
along snow-paths,
your way lit up by
bonfires, while shadows
play among the fir trees,
each with a star at its
tip.

In Russia, the horses
neigh as they pull the
troikas up and down the
towns and race the trains
from Moscow to St Petersburg.
And they snort and steam
and tinkle their bells
and the ice crackles
and the hackles of
wild dogs rise in the
steppe and Rasputin
cackles and sips his
cyanide, while the
skirts of the Romanov
girls whirl and swirl
like snowflakes, and
they huddle to keep
warm and they cuddle
Alexei, the prince with the

sailor hat. And their hands
freeze, and they wheeze
as the surprise bullets
go through them.

Tinderbox

Wild boars blink in the sun. Bolt.
The deer merge with the trees. Birds
fly away between dawn and dusk. Black
spiders dangle and weave. Bunnies
burrow deep. Hornets buzz
between us as we bend
our heads over the map. Blink.
We have lost our bearings
in this atrium of leaf, branch,
twig and trunk.

We cannot find the star-blaze
where the six paths meet. Behold,
I send you forth with your beloved
son. Blinded,
I wait till you disappear over the brink.

The forest catches its breath.
Blanches
when I open the box.
Strike a match. Blow
it out.

Sister Death

Sister Death walks in through the door of my head
jangling her keys, while I'm still in bed.
I say, 'You can stay now. Sit down. Bide your time.
You belong to me fully now. Finally. Mine.'

I wanted to keep you out there in the cold,
to keep you locked out even as I grew old.
I thought if I managed to keep that door shut,
I'd escape death myself, live a deathless life, but

a shadow grew up that attacked me instead,
wrapped me round like a shroud, came to live in my head;
like a dangerous madwoman locked in a cell,
she rattled her shackles and gave me pure hell.

Now that Death has come in and I've got her name,
that Shadow's gone out, and I'm not the same;
no longer resisting, I open my head
to my own Sister Death lying with me, in bed

so close to my body, wherever I go,
till finally, one day, we'll both go below;
but this morning I waken to bird cries and blue,
to frost and fogged windows, and life that is new.

I'm listening to Stabat Mater

I'm listening to Stabat Mater.
The choirs pass by like ships
in full sail under the
cliff of dream. 'To thine
own self be true,' a voice rings
out, piercing me like a
needle. The cats are in
bed. The dog waits for his
supper. The clock whirrs
round on invisible springs,
and the moon hides behind
blackberry clouds, its face
all sticky and smeared.
The veils of the temple are torn.

When mother comes, she will
re-set the pendulums of
hope. I hear words like
'desolate' and see people standing
at the foot of their own
crucifixes or impaled
thereon. Each to his own.
Her own.

I'm listening to Stabat Mater.
The choirs pass by like ships
in full sail, under the
cliff of dream.

I wake up in quicksand

I wake up in quicksand,
hear the heavy feet of night
retreating behind slammed
doors. The day is waiting
to be reinvented. The heavy clay
shapeless on the table of
morning. Dogs are whimpering in the
corners of my mind and desperate
children refuse to go to school.

The nuns come, swaggering, in big
black tents, swinging their monster
beads. The clocks have stopped
ticking. In the silence, I fill my
lungs, the air going down to the very
roots of the world. Something stirs in the
tangled undergrowth of this
new day, something silver
darts around the
corner of wakening,
shattering the dream-mirror.

Suddenly there is light and
oxygen, and the heart picks up its
heavy load and
walks.

Sipping vodka

I speed over the Alps
and look brazenly down;
I glide over cathedrals
of ice. Flying buttresses
rise to meet me. Gargoyles
monkey about. Troglodyte
angels clank by.

Great ships

Great ships like trees in the
back yard, under the star
paths; navigators of the
night. From the top-mast of my
high window, I observe the
currents, and the
winds I know by their
smell. Tonight it's the
east wind, cold and
uneasy. Lost cats
crouch in the branches.
The yew berries have all
been trampled into the
ground. My husband is curled up
in his bunk – his shift is the early
morning. But I am the night watcher.
I call the stars to me and I
name them, each and every one, in
Arabic.

The healing touch

The barrier goes down. It glows red.
OTHER PEOPLE KEEP OUT, or you're dead.

But alone in the therapy room
I weave prayers on my ten-fingered loom.

The white-coated nurses have fled,
observe me through cameras instead.

They've tattooed a few dots on my skin
to show where the beams must go in.

I am raised on my altar of tin
Eli, lama sabachthani. Amen.

The machine hovers over my chest,
at a hair's breadth from me comes to rest.

It embraces me with a strange groan;
I don't budge while the healing goes on.

Now there's silence except for a bleep;
I half-open my eyes, take a peep.

The nurses creep in, realign
a body that's no longer mine.

They are gone before I can say 'Hi!'
Goodbye, Yahweh's angels, goodbye.

The barrier is down. It glows red.
PEOPLE KEEP OUT, or you're dead.

Moult

She kept the other breast. The hair
that had been fair grew back, black.

She found a crop of spuds under her arm.
They gouged them out and with curved needles

darned. Daisies lose their petals
in the scampering winds of May.

The dandelions' lush heads turn into clocks
and then they blow away.

But did you ever hear of 'eclipse plumage'?
Birds moult, you see. They must renew

their feathers every year because of wear
and tear. And wild fowl lose

flight feathers all at once. For six weeks
cannot fly. Some drakes turn into

pulsing sacs of dowdy brown and grey.
Camouflaged as water-hens,

they wedge themselves between the nest and nestlings,
reeds and sedge. Doomed for a season

to a slow decay – like her
(the one who lost the breast) and me

(oh prithee please do not enquire) – they wait
for nature's fledge.

The golden retriever grieves for her mate

The hooded crows roost early now,
November trees are black.
The sun goes down at 4 p.m.
and leaves a blood-stained track.

My antelope, my darling, my gazelle.

We calm her with valerian
and drops of chamomile,
infuse the roots of heliotrope
to soothe her for a while.

My antelope, my darling, my gazelle.

His last night was a rasping breath
that laboured up the stairs
and filled the house, and lodged behind
her sleepless eyes and ears.

My antelope, my darling, my gazelle.

She leans her head against our knees,
she follows us to bed
and lies stretched out upon the floor
as if she, too, were dead.

My antelope, my darling, my gazelle.

Thinking of Emily Dickinson

I could arrange, like her, to wear a snow-white flannel gown,
a violet posy at my throat, and in each hand a fresh-cut
heliotrope.

Six Irishmen could lift me up and bear me out the door,
around the garden, through the barn, across the fields of
    buzzing
buttercups.

If you insist, I'll listen to a passage from the Scriptures
and a prayer. But I must hear most needfully 'Last Lines'
in its entirety,

from Emily Brontë's pen. Then lower me into
eternity – the family plot. Engrave the words 'Called back'
on my small stone,

and on my death cert say my occupation was 'At home'.
I've left great bundles of rough poems with Maggie Maher, my
    maid.
She guards them

in her trunk. But I have ordered her, as literary
executor, to burn the junk. She'll carry out my wishes.
She's great at beds

and fires

and washing dishes.

The dowager queen's 'Te Deum'

And I have sworn before the king, my son,
who is a fool,
that I have never slept with Bishop Alwyn;
nor kissed
the Lord's anointed one, except at Michaelmas
his blessed ring.

King Edward, Sire, although you be my son,
you're but the pawn
of Robert de Jumièges. You give credence
to his tittle-tattle,
lies; ignore your mother's cries
of innocence.

Tomorrow, therefore, I will walk through flame
and clear my name
in Winchester Cathedral. And you,
my sovereign liege,
if God is just, you'll be dishonoured, lose
the people's trust,

receive a thousand lashes of the cane.
Tonight
with Spanish lace upon my head, I keep a vigil
at St Swithin's
tomb. Adumbral centaurs recognize
my pain,

and stone-faced angels hanging in the vault;
and looming griffins,
basilisks with fatal breath; and dragons;
nameless winged
and taloned things that lurk between the cloister
and the slype.

I call to witness husbands, wives, and knights
caparisoned;
and black-swathed nuns, and maidens, merry widows,
tonsured monks,
recumbent figures stretched out on a slab,
that I am not

at fault. Cyclamens grow wild
beyond the walls,
the towering lime-trees drip. Winter waters
gather
in the crypt. The wyvern slythes. At dawn
the whole of England

comes to stare when I take off my shoes,
strip to my shift.
I call upon the God who saved Susanna,
and cross the burning
ploughshares in bare feet. I must admit
that, much to my

surprise, I walk on air. I swoon, I think,
I blaze with light.
I'm onyx, topaz, beryl, jasper, chrysolite.
Edward, the King,
my son, who is a fool, shits on his throne
beside the altar

rail. His great men wring bejewelled hands,
grow pale.
Robert de Jumièges sets sail for France.

Perceval's sister

Who has the loveliest hair in the world?
Whisper, whisper, Perceval's sister.

Who turns it into a belt for a sword?
Ho, hum, said Perceval's sister,
Pellinore's daughter, the holy nun.

Who leads the knights on the path of the Grail?
Whisper, whisper, Perceval's sister.

With eyes like a cat's to light up the trail?
Ho, hum, said Perceval's sister,
Pellinore's daughter, the holy nun.

Who offers her veins to the sharp little knife?
Whisper, whisper, Perceval's sister.

Who fills a bowl with the rose of her life?
Ho, hum, said Perceval's sister,
Pellinore's daughter, the holy nun.

Who came in a ship with sails of milk?
Whisper, whisper, Perceval's sister.

And left in a barge all hung with black silk?
Ho, hum, said Perceval's sister,
Pellinore's daughter, the holy nun.

Who will wait in the ground till it's time to be wed?
Whisper, whisper, Perceval's sister.

Will the hair she cut off grow back on her head?
Ho, hum, said Perceval's sister,
Pellinore's daughter, the holy nun.

Long-distance Swimmer

Hungry for water she lowers herself
into lakes.
She stares at her face in the mere.

Bare but for Speedos and membrane-like cap,
she divines
where to go by a trembling of hands,

follows a ley-line through bog-hole and quarry
and dam.
She hangs Holy Marys on bushes,

she wades through the slobs, descends the dank steps
to the well.
Cheered on by St Gobnait and nine grazing

deer, a badger, an otter, a fox and a
hare,
she dives into rivers, she butterflies

over the weir. She crawls up canals.
Rises and
falls at the lock. When the keeper has

opened the gates with his hydraulic key,
she shakes herself
loose of her togs and her cap.

Her neck disappears. She turns grey. Grows a fur coat
and claws.
Her limbs fuse in a silvery flash

as she swims for dear life out to sea.

November visit

Some go round naked, in the Hallowe'en masks
of their faces.
Some are strapped into giant perambulators.

Ownerless dentures are moaning on bath chairs.
Vacant skulls
gape at the moon. Kitty

is curled on her cushion; the stump of her lost tail
well-bearded
with fur. Tommy is widdling;

his little-boy penis hangs down like a piece
of wet string.
Under his trousers, Father

is wearing a nappy; he stores a zoo-language
deep
in his throat. It's tablets, like Smarties,

for beddy-byes now, and nursie's hand cold
on his brow.
Father peeps through the rails of his cot

at the star-cracker night. The Great Bear, as always,
is prowling
about. The hungry fox waits

at the gate. Orion is pulling the sword
from his belt.
It's too late to go zimmering out.

Strangers come shimmering in through the wall,
move their mouths,
wet the flop of his cheek. Father purses

his lips, blows out words one by one. Like bubbles
they pop
in the air till the strangers go blank,

disappear. 'What to do? What to do?' He dials
nine-nine-nine
on the palm of his hand. He presses

a fist to his ear; hears the Angel of God
on the line.
Outside, the apples

ferment on the trees. Father puts down the phone.
He rests
his great head on his knees.

Prince Lucifer

Prince Lucifer, the great God's darling son; the favourite,
    the loyal one;
the chief of all the angels; the one who wore the sapphired
    crown; the one whose eyes
were bright and dark, the sunset and the morning star;
    the one whose locks lit up
the Northern sky.

Lucifer. Light-bearer. The names of stars his litanies and
    attributes.
A galaxy of light the wonder-hair that sparked and
    glowed, that kindled fires
in icy waste, in frozen steppe. Thus Lucifer the prince
    before his fall.
But when he fell,

when he uprose against his sovereign liege, the god who
    made him, Abba, Father,
Daddy: when Lucifer the prince, betrayed his Father's trust,
he fell from zenith platform, from the heights, from far
    above the sky we see,
and all the earth

went mad awhile, and all the lights went out.

Saint Catherine

After the miracle,
glued to the spot,
an icon in gold-leaf and scarlet,

she strokes the spiked wheel
as she would a pet dog.
The Emperor gapes;
gifts her a necklace, a necklace

of blood. Milk flows
from the miracle head
as it rolls off the block.
Bright as a nimbus it hangs

on the air, bearing
a crown. A crucifix
sprouts in the clasp
of her hands; black as the clay

that sticks to her feet,
beckoning once,
before sucking her in.

Hocus-pocus

Magician by day, he fools her with his hocus-pocus.
Pulls doves from his sleeves, jack-rabbits, Great Danes.
    A touch
of his wand and a baby grows under her smock.

By night a mere man with a cone on his head, he loses
his nerve at the thought of her belly ballooning with child.
He plies her with gin and hot baths; makes her jump

from the top of the stairs. The baby seeps out, disappears
in the sheets. He weeps as mosquitoes whine over the feast.
Strange lizards dart up the walls, slide over

her blood-splattered thighs. He fetches infusions of hyssop
and moistens her lips with a sponge. Turns away to throw up.
He waves his wand – useless at night – dons his star-studded

cape; throws flames from his uvula; thrusts a bright sword
down his throat. Hocus-pocus. The clotted suns rise in a bubble.
Behind the black breast of the chimney, the crickets *cri-cri*.

The crossing

The little boy was feather light, his countenance
amazing bright. I sat him on my shoulder.

He quivered with anticipation of delight
and half of fright as I stepped in the water.

The sky grew dark. The wind whipped up the corners
of my cloak. I leaned upon my staff of knotted

oak. The river rose. It ran full spate. But
as I lunged towards the farther shore,

my spine began to bend and break beneath the toddler's
sudden monstrous weight. I stumbled, pitched

the child into the foam. He, like a millstone,
sank. The whole world shook. I groped for him

with blinded hands, but barely made it back to land,
alone. My gilly-dog, a hound with web-like

paws, and eyes illumed, plunged in
from the high bank. Sucked down by some strange undertow,

he found the leaden child and pulled him out.
I gave the boy the kiss of life, and he was wondrous

haloed all about. 'You cheeky brat',
I cried, 'What were you at? We could have drowned

all three.' 'Forgive me, sir, I made you bear
the sorrows of mankind across the flood,

as well as me.' My gilly-dog bowed low
before his lord. I barely bent my knee

till I looked up and saw the child
nailed to a bloody tree.

FORTY UNPUBLISHED POEMS

Alcossebre

Daylight. Sun-pop and red glow. Apricot lush. Peach-push and cloud-bleed. Mediterranean sunrise. A blood orange on the moving line of the liquid horizon. Low ripple on the water. Sun-path. Path of gleams. Tinsel-toed stepping-stones of sun over salt. Daylight. Sun. *Sol. El sol. Le soleil.* Masculine in every language. Even in Arabic. The sun. *El sol. Le soleil.* Keep rising. Daylight keep coming. From the second floor balcony of the small hotel in Alcossebre, I see the dawn breaking. The deep blue of the Valencian sky and the deeper blue of its sea. *La mar.* Feminine. *In its dress of innocence*, the bloodied sun rises out of the deep. Keep rising. *In its dress of innocence* it shows its face. Darkening the morning star. Casting shadows on the red earth at my feet. The almond trees have long since shed their communion white, their apple-blossom pink. They stand in their bare boughs and their sprinkle of leaf. They stand and wait for the September fruiting. The September fruiting. The autumns of the almond-trees. The nets cast under their branches; and the almond-gatherers with their long poles thwacking, thwacking, thwacking; knocking down the almond-clusters. And gathering their catch in the low-slung nets. Nets. Green and brown nets spread out on the red ground and pulled in to the sides of tractors and loaded onto trailers and brought to the town for shelling. All night the sound of almonds popping out of their shells. Peasants in doorways, cracking the nuts. Shells under your feet as you walk down to the Montemar for dinner. A smell of almond hanging in the warm air. You sit at a table beside the window that opens onto the sea. The fishermen out in their boats with big lamps for night fishing. Each boat with its own sun, its globe of white light. Each boat with its own glow.

Under the high glitter of stars, the fishing boats are like comets on the curve of the sea. Silent. Their tails a sparkle of netted fish. The boats swirl across the horizon till daybreak. Day pops open with the crack of an almond shell and I am there once again on the balcony to see the night's fruit, solid as a nut, move into its fiery groove where the ocean tilts. All day the red sun glides along its track, up and over my head; the blinding wheel gathering momentum as it rolls again down the curve of metallic blue and lands on the feathery sea, bursting like an overripe tomato and staining the whole sky with its pulp.

I

The thing is to get into water.
Salt water slaking the heat.
The beat of waves under the tin-can
sun, flashing silver into the corners
of my eyes. The skies too blue to bear.

Bare bodies, nut-coloured, tanned,
span Alcossebre shoreline.
Bikini-lines and rhyming breasts.
Such breasts. And buttocks tucked
round the back of every belle
and beau. Or twinned in the sun.

And babies sitting in hollows;
in water-filled holes; in sun hats,
splashing with buckets and spades.
Buckets and spades.

The castles. You should have seen
the castles. Turrets and moats. Flags.
High walls. Shell windows. Curves
and dimples. Wimples of sun around
all the faces. Warming themselves
against the sky.

The sigh rising up from the awnings,
the intakes of breath, the yawnings.
And Abel in his Moroccan skin,
thin as a rake. His laugh. His tight
curls. His teeth white as peeled
almonds. His rolled 'r's rippling
in waves. The prevailing wind dragging
his broken Spanish across the sand
like an old bucket. And finally,

the Tramontana, the Mistral, the Cierzo,
call it what you like, blowing up
the mountain to El Pinar where all the gabble
is in German or Catalan or English
with a Dublin accent. Three Molloys
on top of a hill in Castellón.

The first one a man, his head full of tunes
and his fiddle muted with a clothes peg.
The other two, women, warm
with memories of Barcelona
until the blind dates that left thumb-marks
like bruises on the calendar of both lives.

2

These sandals have walked in Spain.
Have burned on the pavements of Valencia.
Melted on the hot plates under my feet.
They have walked on wet sand in Alcossebre
after the hot, showery, feathery precipitation
they call rain.

They have meditated under the white
counterpane of my narrow bed
in Tossalet; deciphering crickets:
crickets chattering and humming like dervishes
through the spinny nights of xafago;
the pool listless in its blue perfection;
the swings under the pungent pines
motionless, moping, waiting for the weight
of children, the high pipe of voices.
The swings, lumpy in the night,
without their burdens.

Now I've lost my sandals and
I am walking barefoot
on the red tiles, on the hot sand;
I am walking into the boisterous sea,
the silver and turquoise waves
knocking me backwards into the soft
hollows under the water.

The cradles of Alcossebre. The cradles
in the dunes. And I see the pregnant
German woman in her flowing crimson dress,
her light and airy dress, her billowy dress,
sitting in the four-square chair,
heavy in the sand.

And she is leaning back into the sun.
Her long nails are blood red. Her wrists
are thick with gold bangles. She has called
a flaxen-haired toddler to her. The child
is naked. They speak in thick sounds,
sounds that lack the airiness of Castilian,
but approximate the density and sponginess
of Catalan: all soft 'g's and 'j's
and scrunched consonants.

Now I'll tell you a story.
All the Catalan babies know it.
'The little ship sails out to sea.
The captain sails out to sea.'

And if you're bored with that one,
here's the other one about the 'patufet'.

'Where are you, little lad, little lad?'
'In the cow's belly where it neither snows
nor rains.' And the chorus, which every Catalan
child knows: 'Patim, patam, patum,
men and women with heads held high,
patim, patam, patum,
do not step on the little lad.'

3

The strange and lovely beach of Alcossebre
on a windy day with the sun turning the tumbling
waves to silver. Blinding silver waves
digging holes in the sand, under the water.

So, when you walk carefully into the sea,
you find you are going down steps of sand,
and tumbling into sand pits and sand hollows.
And all the time the waves are buffeting round you
like white and silver flags, knocking you down.

And you find a friendly hole in the sand
under the water and you sit on the edge
of your sand tub and the waves come fluttering
round your neck like a ruff.

And you cannot see your hands or feet
under the sandy waves. Millions of golden
particles are flying around you as in a wild
washing-machine window; and all you see is sand
like gold-leaf in smithereens; spinning like mad
between you and your hands, between you and your feet.

And you feel the pull, the under-tow, of the whipped-up
sea, dragging you this way and that
towards the town and towards the mountains
and towards the Balearic Islands, out of sight.

And you are at the centre of a glass world,
round and heavy. And someone is shaking you
like mad; and water thick with gold dust
is densing you all around; turning your hair
bright as an angel's, your skin luminous
mirroring back the sun.

Your hands and feet are weightless, and foam
ruffles round your body; now high, now low,
like whipped cream, like golden Pavlova
meringue. And someone has placed a few grains
of salt on your tongue; and shattering out
from the encircling glass, you rise
as in a baptism or resurrection, into a world
that is pure blue, where you are transformed
utterly and forever. Amen.

4

Those waves that get you by the ankles with vicious
little swirls and pull you into sandy depths;
whirlpools of grit spinning up and round you,
clouding your view of your feet. Those undertows
that pull you out of your standing and suck you
horizontally through glassy sheets of flat water.

Those sudden hollows in the sand, as you paddle
aimlessly, staring at shells through the transparent
water; those sudden hollows, miniature dells,
vales, scoops in the floor of the sea; and you lose
your grip and you bumpsa-daisy: salt
water tingling your wide-open eyes.

And other times you're swimming along and suddenly
a huge wave, elephantine, trunk snorting and spouting,
has you in its soft grey clutches and you thrash around
wildly in search of a platform, a surface solid
enough to take your darting toes.

Another time you're lying on your back, doing
the Dead Man's Float, the Dead Woman's Float,
and thinking about nothing. Bits of seaweed slither
past, touching you lightly. You squeeze and spot the soft
globular bits, squishing out the gel and breathing in
the smell of iodine. And every now and then you splash

your feet up and down, up and down, moving yourself
over a little bit under the sky, inspecting a new cloud.

And sometimes you might be almost dropping off,
kindly, in the soft Mediterranean air, when
your husband, boyfriend, lover, dives in on top
of you, all male panache and boxer shorts, and rumbles
you over and over; and the water gets up your nose,
the dragging waves pull at your bikini,
and the seaweed tickles you behind the ears.
It's hilarious.

But it takes a while for the rocking to slow down,
slow down, slow down, and for you to regain your
poise, so that you can light-foot it out
eventually onto the hot sand, with your usual cool.

5

In Alcossebre it's different. The stars are gentle here
and the sky soft in its blackness. There is a quiet surrendering
of the sun and an imperceptible sliding away of light.

Suddenly you are aware of cicadas, and the smell of the red earth
cooling. And under the dark green leaves of the orange trees
small night-creatures stir. Flurries of wild barking
punctuate your sleep, and you go out in bare feet to the balcony
and look down at the sea.

Phosphorescence twinkles even at this distance, and you know
that the next day those waves will be pounding at your feet.
And you will be looking at the sun through the
    churned-up water
of your own splashing. And the waves will keep coming in.

And they like to trick you, running towards you from
    several directions
at once. And sometimes you see the sun shining directly
    through a swathe
of water, like a pillar of light coming towards you. And the
    pale blue,
turquoise, milky-green water, rimmed with silver, smooth
as a bangle, moves towards you like butter. And you slide
through it laughing, and shake the golden drops from your
    skin and out of your hair.
And you've salt on your tongue. And you turn around to wave
    at your lover.
And another butter wave slides past. And you cut through
    this one
with ease. And you want to be left alone to play with the sea.

The almond gatherers

With long poles they thwack
at the trees. Nuts plummet
onto the netted ground.

The red earth rattles,
and turns brown.

Tractors drag the crops into town
and the shelling starts. Husks explode
like shrapnel under our feet.

A smell of marzipan rises
out of the dust.

Animal rights

They don't know they are old.
The nights are darker now. The days are cold. The very orbit
of the earth has slowed.

They don't know they are dying.
They just lie there, wait for you to do what you must do.
They know that you are trying.

The baker of Baghdad

I wear an apron flapping like a tent,
a cap, a paper boat, upon my head,
and through these endless ricocheting nights
you'll find me white as flour,
making bread.

Day after bombed-out day deep in my bunker
I pummel dough and wait for it to swell,
I tell my worry beads, down on my hunkers,
and slide black trays into the mouth
of hell.

Up on the streets the US 'screaming eagles'
are battling with the sons of all the tribes
whose weapons of destruction are not guns
but Holy Books and catapults,
and knives.

A sandstorm comes as Allah shakes his cloak,
gives mosque and market square a sheen of gold.
The citizens emerge, do I see ghosts?
their ululations make my blood
run cold.

The sirens on the minarets whine up,
or is it just the evening call to prayer?
I stoke the fires until the yeast ferments,
explodes just like a bomb in
the hot air.

The flour bags are empty now. The water running
low. With rolling pins as big as tanks
I'm eking out the dough. I've joined the
underground *mujahideen*. I'm on my own
jihad.

The bearded lady speaks

My mother was a ballerina,
petite in her pliés, her pas de deux.

People queued to see her pirouette;
now they queue to gawk at me.

It's a dollar a peep behind the flap
of the circus tent. I pose

in my tutu and my pumps. Plié,
pas de deux. Mother sits

in her cubicle and rakes
the money in. I am the Sugar Plum

Fairy and The Dying Swan.

Crying-bowls of silk

Crying-bowls of silk
White as milk

Crying-bowls of gold
Growing cold

Crying-bowls of clay
For every day.

Damaged at birth

Damaged at birth which sliced off the top
of his head, he wore his hair long; wired his numb
skull to the moon. Tall as a telegraph
pole, brittle ankles, black boots, he softened
himself with old hand-knitted jerseys, turf-brown
corduroys.

He made himself worse with the little green apples
he stole. Then he missed lots of school. Lug-musician,
he only could strum on his Spanish guitar,
his hard nails like plectrums, white fingers *cejillas*
that pressed on the strings while he hummed a strange tune.
Gifted child

giving Fascist salutes at his first and his last
summer camp. 'Viva Franco.' They hoisted the flag.
'Arriba España', he muttered when they pulled it
down. Dead relatives turned in their graves.
His eyes hard as marbles, they flicked between hazel
and brown.

Home once again Mamma stuffed him with *churros*
and chocolates, expressed the warm milk from her breasts,
tried to fill out his white hollow cheeks; pump up
his cherry-red lips. They put themselves forward
to guzzle and slurp, to purse, and to siphon
hot sops.

Entrepreneur, as a boy, he rented out comics;
the profits he stashed in a chamber pot under
the bed – the pot with the all-seeing eye.
He crawled in due season with uncles and aunts
under bushes, filled baskets and buckets with strawberries,
mushrooms,

counted the cash at the registers down
in the town. By dint of hard practice, he taught himself
music from records, like 'Nights in the Gardens
of Spain'. He played the guitar at fiestas
and drove women wild with his black hair all over
his face, señoritas,

señoras. He even awakened the passions
of grown men, and boys. He singled me out.
Then wafted me up through a ceiling of cloud
to visit the Virgin of Snow in her icy-blue gown.
He took me to cinemas,

gave me the *Sugus* to suck, fruity Chupa Chups,
tiny wrapped sweets. We drank the small glasses
of wine. He gave me an angel to pin on my
pastel-striped gown. He bent down to kiss me,
he lied, said he'd miss me, went off with his Lady
Guitar.

After the concert, the standing ovation, elated
we watched as the blood-orange sun submerged

itself in the blue sea. He invited the girl with
the pale Flemish breasts that popped out when her halter neck
broke to be with him at dawn. And not me.
I found my dark voice,

my dark laugh when I left him. And he gnashed his little sharp
teeth. They told me he smashed his guitar,
stamped his feet and lay down on the floor. He bawled
for his Mamma. She knelt on all fours and fed him
from pendulous breasts. He guzzled and slurped,

latched on with his Cupid's bow lips. He siphoned
hot sops.

For Bracken (3 months' mind)

Tonight I place upon your roof of clay
A little boat, a bell, a bowl of water,
A single candle to light up your way.

It's three months since you left, but let me say
This silver bracelet, made for Jairo's daughter,
Tonight I place upon your roof of clay.

Your golden friend and I have come to pray
And whisper to you by the grassy altar;
A single candle lights us on our way.

While it still burns we are allowed to stay
Beside you, so your steps may never falter.
Tonight I place upon your roof of clay

My own sad weight. Come back without delay –
But if you can't, you know I'll join you later;
A single candle will light up my way.

We've changed the clocks to winter time today,
Three seasons gone now, in this year's last quarter.
I place upon your sacred roof of clay
A single candle to light up your way.

Foundation garment

I sit in my corset, pink,
stroking the whale bone.

Trapped in my closet
(where I am most at home)

I cosset my stays, hold in
my breath. Faint.

Four Haiku

Knickerbockers, puffs
of lace, flounce on Sally's legs,
swing from her pegs, bounce.

*

Flaming maple trees
in autumn, tongues of fire on
altars of dark wood.

*

Silent as a cat's
the flit across the street at
midnight: urban fox.

*

Still as steeples they
stand, gazing into rock pools,
herons poised to pounce.

Going, going, game

On Mondays
I'm mute.

On Tuesdays
I chatter.

On Wednesdays
I whimper.

On Thursdays
I throw up.

On Fridays
I fidget.

On Saturdays
I sit in my apron
and stare.

On Sundays
I put my head
in the gas oven.

He prefers other people's mimosas

He prefers other people's mimosas,
their villas in Spain, their neuroses,
their books (antiquarian),
locks (Rastafarian),
he prefers other people's mimosas.

Holding and folding

Holding and folding the fine sheets of words into verse,
Inviting the friend in, just carefully setting the table,
Whatever the effort, chaos and madness be worse.

Planting the bulbs, spending each coin in your purse,
Clearing the weeds back, making a space, you're well able,
Holding and folding the fine sheets of words into verse.

Each present moment, nones, vespers, matins and terce,
Mythologize, fairy tale, parable, chatter and fable,
Whatever the effort, chaos and madness be worse.

Pick all those pole-beans, take a hot bath, just immerse,
Be your own mother and father, hop into your cradle
Holding and folding the fine sheets of words into verse.

Sleep with the cat, with the lover, your bottle, your nurse,
Gibber and jabber, stream along in your own tower of Babel,
Whatever the effort, chaos and madness be worse.

Rattle your tin, before you're cast off in your hearse,
Be your bright self; just scoop yourself up in your ladle,
Holding and folding the fine sheets of words into verse
Whatever the effort, chaos and madness be worse.

The house has become strange

The house has become strange.
The doors don't fit.
Water pours from the ceilings
and a putrid smell
is pushing its way through solid concrete
under our feet.

The morning sky is full of warnings
and the men are on their way.
With pick-axes and sharp-edged shovels they come,
digging holes big as graves
at the four corners of our house.

I built myself a harbour

I built myself a harbour made of granite
With cunning steps and lighthouse fiercely flashing
For I am weak and vulnerable, dammit.

I gave away my luck

I wore black rings under my eyes,
widow's rags in the street
when Julio died.

For thirteen years I kept away
from men. Ramón walked
under my balcony every day.

For thirteen years his whistling
wafted up, wore me down.
Oh my God.

I wore white for the wedding:
new bride at forty-one.
My son gave me away

against his will. I showered him
with trinkets from the cake:
bells, horseshoes, cats.

I gave away my luck.

*

Ramón loosened his tie
but the knot in his throat
was still there when he dropped:

his mouth wide with surprise,
his eyes glued to the ceiling.
We waked him that night,

laid him out on the bed
in his suit. The whole village
gawked. Someone propped up

his chin; put two coins
on his lids. The priest
oiled him and breathed

in his ear: Oh my God.

*

Two days later at noon
the funeral proceeds
down the street: men fore

women aft. In black rags,
set adrift among hankies
and skirts, I cling

to the rope of my beads.
In the church it's men right,
women left. Oh my God.

*

At the cemetery, Paco,
the caretaker, climbs up
the ladder, breaks open

the family niche;
scoops out the old bones,
lays them under the trees.

We gape at the skulls:
jut of chin, slope of brow,
the who's who of the dead.

Is that Julio, Concha
or Juan? Is it Grandma?
Oh God. Whistling low,

Paco bundles the lot
into bags; shoves them right
to the back of the niche

with his pole, tidies up
with his dustpan and brush.
In a sweat at the top

of the ladder, he shouts:
'Now heave-ho with Ramón'.
Raised on four pairs of shoulders,

the fresh coffin slides
into place. Paco buffs up
the cross, his chamois

runs over the wood;
then he walls Ramón in.
Bricks and mortar,

a tap of his trowel
and a quick RIP
just in case.

     *

Next day Paco, the caretaker,
comes to my door,
bills and coos; pecks my cheek,

looks deep in my eyes,
tries to bury his face
in my hair. 'A smidgin

of hope, I beg you,
María', he weeps.
I push him away.

'Are you mad?' Paco pulls out
the ring. 'Thirteen years
in my pocket, María.

Here, see if it fits.'
He slips the gold band
on my finger. 'Oh love

of my life.' I grow faint.
Ramón stares from the black and white
photograph nailed

to the wall. He speaks
through my mouth. 'Get out, Paco,
you bastard. Out. Out.

I'm still warm in my box.'
White as a ghost,
Paco turns on his heel.

The ring falls to the ground.
They find him next day
mown down by the train

from Madrid. Oh love
of my life. My cheeks
are destroyed with mascara,

my mouth's a red blob.
The town's full of blab.
My son comes to visit,

eyes cold as ice,
'Nice one, Mamma', he blurts.
'What's that, a new ring?'

I bless myself quick,
pinch of salt, rabbit's foot,
I wear my bride's gown

inside out. If my luck
doesn't turn, I'll follow
my Paco. I'll catch

the next train to Madrid.
Oh my God.

I lived in Spain

I lived in Spain for fifteen years, but then
I found my heart was like an empty room;
I packed my bags and went back home again.

I left the ancient street, the small cramped den,
Dismantled all the threads of my fine loom;
I lived in Spain for fifteen years, but then

The one I loved abandoned me, that's when
The sun alone could not dispel the gloom;
I packed my bags and went back home again.

The things I lost I can't tell with my pen –
The Spanish sounds and smells, I can't resume;
I lived in Spain for fifteen years, but then

I left it all – my hope, my secret plan,
The damp squib of your love, the burst balloon;
I packed my bags and went back home again.

It took me much too long to say 'Amen',
To turn true north and claim my own heirloom.
I lived in Spain for fifteen years, but then
I packed my bags and went back home again.

I'll gather fruits

Today I struggled with a cloud
that wrapped me round just like a shroud
and tried to stifle me
within a gloom.

But life came creeping round the edge
of my impenetrable hedge
and held me like a glass
up to the light.

Today will be a wonder day;
I'll gather fruits along the way
and place them in the basket
of my soul.

I'm a full-blooded woman

I'm a full-blooded woman, I am, I am,
my cheeks are ever so red,
and if you dare to come with me
you'll see what I'm like in bed.

I can see the steam rising as I speak,
the glister of sweat on my brow;
if you think that I've had enough, man, my dear,
sure, I'm only warming up now!

In Guadalupe

the old Cathedral tilts
in the plaza. Mariachis
trumpet in the heat.

Mary wilts behind bulletproof glass
while the manic roses
of the miracle cloak
climb up the wall.

Stubborn as sun-baked adobe,
Mexicans, on bloody knees,
drag themselves to the shrine.

Mad for another miracle,
a crazed *campesino*
is loading his gun.

Keeping the warm animal

Keeping the warm animal of the
heart snug; feeding it
good things; letting it love –
this is what you were born for.

Letting the heart follow its own
steady beat, placing no boulders in its
way, no ice. Keeping the music
playing. And the silence
between.

Keeping the dreams topped up,
the fear low. Trusting in a
mystery that holds the world
together, the stars in their
places, even while we sleep,
even while we ignore them.

Breathing the breath that
sustains us, even in sleep.
Trusting the body that keeps us
alive, even while we sleep.
Keeps us alive while the mind
somersaults and
feelings run rampant. Even while
dreams heal and nightmares
purge.

Trusting the body that roots us
here, in this world, our home
country; our feet walking its
earth; the heart beating its
beat, even when I forget who I am.

A letter to someone no longer in my life

I am no longer proud
to wear the shroud
that you bequeathed to me.

When tragedy was in fashion
then my passion
was to feel unfree.

Locked in the chains
of unrequited love, the flames
consuming me

Like some bright Joan of Arc
upon the pyre
I loved the fire.

But I did not become a saint
and resurrect
that would be incorrect.

I lived for my addiction
my affliction
was my secret raison d'être.

But now I write this letter
just to say I'm feeling better
without you.

PS Please find enclosed
the winding-cloth
along with all the froth
you gave to me.

Memory jolts

Memory jolts. Flashes of pink
in the brain. Violet stripes on the wall
and purple lines painted on carpets that lead
to the hall.

In the back of beyond the old cats are playing,
slow-motion praying, sinking on haunches
like sphinxes with curlicued nails. The swirlicued
horns of the ram.

Cushions on floorboards. Lairs full of smells.
Sharp nostrils flair at the moon. Out of sight
the retractable genitals, gilded and sore.
Testosterone treated, the males.

My mother wails 'Daughter, oh daughter, they're going
to slaughter the woolly-brained lambs'. Much good
that it does when the trays come around. Marietta
and tea.

In the garden, those leaves, blooming great things
to cover pudenda and tail. Apple cores
litter the ground, birds pick with the gold
of their beaks.

Iodine. Mercurochrome. Syrup of figs.
Soundless as time that sweeps at my face
with its thin metal hands. Loud as the spade
that cuts into loam

on the day that will come. *Carpe diem*, they say
and pray their Novenas, move heaven and earth
with their lips. Firm down the clay.

Mother

Mute, she sits at the table,
telling her beads.
They rattle on
for decades.

She leans into her prayer book.

Under the bellows of her faith,
the gilt-edged pages blaze.

Jolted awake by the clatter
of cups in the kitchen
and the prospect of tea and cake,
she cuts her trimmings short;
rolls her beads, like a handful of nuts,
into her pocket.

The music man succeeds in telling the truth

He eats half a cow before he can speak, drinks
till a tide of blood runs in his cheek, takes out his dark
violin.

He plays a slow air for a year and a day, his shoulders
bent over the task. Then he plucks on a gut string and saws
through his heart.

Nutrient pollution in Lake Chapala

The lake in remote Mexico
is choked with water hyacinths.
It sits in its own juices
like a thick-tufted rug.

Two Indians need to fish,
push their dug-out through the tangle.
From the tuck of hollowed trunk,
hack their way across the water.

Paddles, like machetes, clear
a path towards the light.

The oars on the boat moved

The oars on the boat moved as if hypnotised
towards the island in the centre of the lake.
The transparent woman, somnambulating,
drifted across the little granite harbour,
through the copse, to the burial mound.
Gathering wild roses (they seemed to pick
themselves) she circled the sacred ground,
only her long black hair visible, as she
keened, and tore at her face, over the grave.

But when the monastery bell rang out,
bouncing across the water like a skipping-stone,
she turned, scattering the blood roses in her
haste, and threaded her way back
through the trees, to the coracle. Her hair
became transparent again, in tune with her
body, as she slumped in the bottom of the
boat. And *the oars moved as if hypnotised,*
compelling her back to the tabernacles of
gold on the far shore.

Poem using some images from May Swenson

Earth will not let go our foot
The foot I share with you, dear,
We're gripped deep down just like a root
I hope I've made this clear, dear.

The dreamy thimble on our head
The head I share with you, dear,
Keeps out the sun, the moon instead
Marks out our path, that's clear, dear.

When teeth were tools and life was rough
Our fingers were all frozen, dear,
But you'll recall that little muff
Where our shared hand endured, dear.

When in the bend of our soft mouth
Blue murder lurked betimes, dear,
We simply put away that pout
And our sharp teeth relaxed, dear.

But when it came to deeper things,
Like seas unfolding scrolls, dear,
We found we were two separate beings
With two quite different souls, dear.

We looked into our deep recesses
Thinking one heart to find there
That was the worst of our excesses,
For two hearts lurked behind, dear.

Our hearts were wave-shaped dunes, I found,
I hope I make this clear, dear,
And from our beaks streamed a thin sound
The cry of our despair, dear.

So let's not stand around no more
Lamenting, looking stupid,
Let's go and throttle that sly guy,
The curly-headed Cupid.

He told us lies that we believed
At least we did share that, dear,
But now the colour of the air
In Florence is what matters, dear.

Race to the veterinary hospital

She wanted to go with him. Jump
into the boot where he lay prone.
Run, Sally, run.

I grabbed her by the scruff and looped the choke chain
round her neck as you drove off.
Run, Sally, run.

She dragged me halfway down the lane, her paws insane,
churning the gravel up.
Run, Sally, run.

Your car a distant drone, it took another
tug-of-war to get her home.
Run, Sally, run.

Somewhere between the harbour and the pier
his heart gave out.
Run, Sally, run.

You clutched, de-clutched, changed gear.
She turned to stone.
Run, Sally, run.

Rats scrabble in the roof

Rats scrabble in the roof above my head.
They copulate. I hear their thump and clatter.
They're at it every night when I'm in bed.

They squeeze through granite walls I've heard it said
Through needles' eyes, and drainage pipes, what matter?
Rats scrabble in the roof above my head.

Rigor mortis at Earlsfort Terrace

The student doctors thought we'd like to peep
at stiffs laid out on trolleys in the lab:
cadavers lolling under plastic sheets.

They showed us body parts in jars on shelves:
curved kidneys, disconnected bits of gut,
a brain, a lung, a pancreas, a heart.

You tried to kiss me. But I shied away
from rows of blue-grey foetuses in phials;
your luscious lips could not block out their cries.

Sacromonte

I do not want to go to Sacromonte;
I do not want to go to Gypsy Hill;
I dreamt there was a gypsy dancer up there,
a gypsy who would bend me to his will.

You said I was obsessed with the subconscious;
you said 'Put on your new dress with the frill';
you whistled for a taxi and you took me
to the gypsy who would bend me to his will.

In whitewashed caves we watched the gypsies dancing.
In whitewashed caves we sipped the wine until
it seemed to me each dark-eyed man I looked at
was the gypsy who would bend me to his will.

'Voilà', my husband said, 'all stuff and nonsense';
'Voilà', I nodded, but I glanced round still;
I knew that in the caves of Sacromonte
a come-on from a gypsy's eyes could kill

the marriage vows I made when I was twenty,
the marriage vows I signed with ink and quill
when, before I dreamt of gypsies in Granada,
I looked you in the eye and said 'I will.'

With great relief I saw the show was over.
With great relief I saw you pay the bill,
then out of nowhere came another gypsy,
an old man in worn shoes but with what skill,

he let go of his feet, *zapateando*;
he let go of his hands, the *castañuelas*
commotioning like birds behind his back.
He kept them there; he made the wild birds trill.

He made me mad for love. With his brown hands
he made me mad for love. 'A summer thrill'
my husband said, but I was gone,
with the gypsy who would bend me to his will.

Sea change

I nearly drowned the day you clung to me,
Your arms noosed round my neck, you pulled me down;
Since then I've had a phobia of the sea;

Best friends with water when I was let be
In races, galas, won a small renown;
I nearly drowned the day you clung to me.

You gripped my hips and trapped me with your knee
And wrapped the water round me like a gown;
Since then I've had a phobia of the sea.

You nailed me to the waves as to a tree;
Hysterical, I windmilled like a clown;
I nearly drowned the day you clung to me.

You nearly drowned the moment I got free;
Your sister pulled you out by your wet crown;
Since then I've had a phobia of the sea.

I swapped the ocean for my liberty
And lost my ease with salt and water brown;
I nearly drowned the day you clung to me
Since then I've had a phobia of the sea.

The seer of Tremvan

When J. Gwenogvryn Evans first came across
the Ancient Books of Wales, he comprehended
not a jot, and shelved the lot.

At thirty – after failed careers as businessman
and schoolmaster and priest – he lost his voice,
got pulmonary TB.

He travelled round the world by sea to boost his health.
Kitten-weak, on his return, he dragged himself
to hear the lectures of Professor

Rhys; discovered what he needed now
to do. For forty years, obsessively,
he worked on new transcriptions

of Welsh manuscripts and brought out, by subscription,
immaculate editions (diplomatic
and facsimile) at his own press

in Tremvan, Llanbedrog; so appeared
– on handmade paper, linen, vellum, toned, antique,
with emblematic dragons

on the frontispiece and triple harps and leeks –
*The Red Book Mabinogion, The Black Book
of Carmarthen*, the Codex

of Welsh Laws. Haunted by the harmonies
that he half-glimpsed when leafing through the *Book of
Taliesin* and taunted by

philologists who deemed the poems worthless,
too corrupted by a string of scribal hands
to ever understand,

J. Gwenogvryn Evans ventured out
to see if he could make the garble yield
the spirit of the poet

trapped within. He tidied up the metre,
the orthography, the little lucid bits.
Out of the mists (it seemed to him)

came landmarks (topographical, historical).
In search of clues he spent his summers on the prowl
in Flint and Denbigh. Chased by the bull

of Crugion down on Severnside he saved his pelt
by lepping over gorse and heather, blackthorn bushes,
ditches, stiles, and rusty eight-barred

gates. He walked the English borderlands.
He climbed the hills, surveyed the scene from promontory
fort and castle, Breiddin, Berwyn,

Rhodwydd, Treidden. Bicycled a thousand miles
to see what Taliesin had seen, to feel
what he had felt. It took him seven

years to grip 'The Book'. Then he restored
the text, provided a translation
into English – a beautiful

creation in itself – expounded new
hypotheses, fantastical, and backed them up
with copious and solipsistic

notes. 'And now that I have done my level
best with Taliesin, I'll publish
and be damned'. What matter

that he thought *The Book of Taliesin* was written
by one man? What matter that he thought the poems
belonged exclusively

to Norman times? J. Gwenogvryn Evans,
in setting free the ancient prophet, wizard, mystic,
bard, released himself.

He got no accolades, no gift from kings
(as Taliesin had done); no horses, mantles,
brooches, bracelets, yellow-hilted

swords or golden rings.

Soft target

The cluster bomb exploded underneath the ass and cart.
Stars burst

between the shafts. They showed the donkey's body parts on
    Sky TV.
The US Army

PR guy said 'No. Not we. Not we.'

The creature had no time to feel alarm. He did not bray.
But locals swear

an after-roar hung in the air for days. The polished hooves
that walked

the desert ways are souvenirs of war. A ripped-off ear
is someone's

lucky charm.

Spayed

The vet put her uterus
and ovaries in a jar
for me to see. But
I averted my gaze.

At my next check-up
the gynaecologist peered
through his speculum
and quipped:

'It's all gotta come out, OK?
ASAP.
Of course, it will depend
on how attached you are . . .'

His white coat stared
at me.

Talking legs

You hold your secrets in your legs. They show
The heart, the pain, you won't wear on your sleeve,
In purple veins and bloody wells they glow.

In swishing pools of tender flesh they flow,
In silence their embroideries they weave.
You hold your secrets in your legs. They show

In swollen ankle and arthritic toe.
Beneath the surface all is sob and heave,
In purple veins and bloody wells they glow.

Why urgent ulcers ooze we do not know,
Will never know what nightmares to you cleave,
You hold your secrets in your legs. They show

In lesions on your heels which never go,
In tortured spawgs which no-one can relieve,
In purple veins and bloody wells they glow.

In triple wraps of bandages you sew
The things you loved and lost and mourn and grieve,
You hold your secrets in your legs. They show
In purple veins and bloody wells they glow.

Villanelle of the Bilbao babies

The babies in Bilbao love their bangles,
They lie in prams that are festooned with lace;
Among the frothy wraps you hear the jangles.

Their fingers are all ringed in golden fangles
And tiny chains keep all those rings in place;
The babies in Bilbao love their bangles.

Their curly hair is combed and free of tangles,
The medals round their necks fill them with grace;
Among the frothy wraps you hear the jangles.

Their nannies, stiff with starch, don't get in wrangles,
They push the stately prams with steady pace;
The babies in Bilbao love their bangles.

Their tiny lobes weighed down with glints and dangles,
Dark eyes illuminate each shining face;
Among the frothy wraps you hear the jangles.

My heart is squashed by twenty-seven mangles
As memories of Bilbao round me race;
The babies in Bilbao love their bangles,
Among the frothy wraps you hear the jangles.

Waiting

Outside my kitchen door
on the raised bed
raindrops glitter
in the elephantine leaves
of winter-sprouting broccoli.
The dark purple hearts
are pushing through
stems thick as
rhubarb.

In the March sky
seagulls fling themselves
from cloud to cloud,
the trampoline of the
heavens dense with
feathers.

Down at the Forty Foot
seals play with
winter swimmers
sliding over their salty
napes, tickling them with
their immense
whiskers.

Up in my jacaranda tree,
I tune my dulcimer and
wait for summer. Yellow

earrings dangle from my pale
lobes, but I still wait.

Outside my kitchen door
on the raised bed
raindrops glitter
in the elephantine leaves
of winter-sprouting broccoli.
The dark purple hearts
are pushing through
stems thick as
rhubarb.

The loneliness of Catherine the Great

1

Initially I settled for that nitwit,
Peter Holstein, heir to the Russian throne.
But eight years into marriage, my hymen still
intact, I tired of waiting in the bridal

suite for him to come. Remember that
when just a girl in Stettin, under mother's
roof, I galloped on my pillows, could not
sleep till I was out of puff.

But Peter liked to play in bed with his toy sword
and gun. And as we lay a foot apart,
he drilled his soldiers on the eiderdown;
pretended to shoot dead the little men

of wood and wax and lead.

2

He courted Miss Lopoukhi, just for fun.
And while he fiddled in the drawing room,
I tiptoed out to tryst with Andrew Chernichev,
throw snowballs in the park. Elizabeth,

the Empress, barked at me, sent my beloved
away. Appointed Semenovna

Choglokov, the stupid bitch, to be my watchdog,
shadow, chaperone. Andrew wrote

to me. His letters in the post box sleeves
of wardrobe maids from Finland, delivered as I
sat on the commode. For my replies
I bought a silver pen. We never met again.

3

Andrew's cousin, Zachary, made eyes at me.
I fanned his flame with *billets-doux* between
the minuets. I left my door ajar,
but when he loomed by guarded candlelight

I thought I saw the Empress' face balloon
upon the wall and I took fright. I dared not
let him in. He went back to his regiment.
I lost my bloom, my *joie de vivre*. Refused

to leave my room.

4

The doctor bled me with a dozen leeches.
The Empress sent her confessor to preach at me.

A secret palace clique arranged for Saltikov,
Serguei, a married man, to take me,

impregnate me, make an heir for Russia's sake
(as Peter said: 'I neither wish nor can.')

5

Head-over-heels in love at twenty-five,
I called Serguei 'handsome as the dawn'.
Alas! his passion ended with a yawn,
for I miscarried twice. He didn't give

a fart about my heart; left me the day our
bastard-child was born. The Empress took
my son. I wiped my eyes and donned my favourite
gown, the blue and gold. *Mon Dieu*, but I was

cold. Till my next lover fell into my arms.

6

Everything Serguei had taught me, I passed on
to Poniatovski, darling Stanislaus,
a virgin Pole. He shed his wig and overcoat,
to swim the moat and scale the walls and steal into

my bed. Became the father of my second
child. My husband, Peter, wild for
Lizaveta Vorontsova, didn't give
a damn. The Empress, though, had other plans.

Sent Stanislaus away. And ordered him,
as future King of Poland, designate,
to find a bride of Polish stock, a Catholic
to boot, which I was not. Our baby, Anna,

died at fifteen months. Alone, no one to
hold, my keening filled the Russian steppe,
reached Stanislaus in Warsaw long before
the written word, through icy Vilnius,

Vitebsk and Minsk.

7

I summoned Orlov, Gregory, to be my
adjutant. Lieutenant, Count, a giant of
a man, he proved himself an athlete
in the bed (as they had said). The Empress died.

And Russia nearly fell apart when Peter,
half-deranged, became the Czar. But Orlov,
with my brooch pinned to his heart, arranged a coup
and did him in (for love of country therefore not a

sin) and set me on the throne where I
belonged. Six months' pregnant with his child
on coronation day, I gave him diamonds,
gold, and silken clothes; got up his nose

when I refused to marry him. To keep the palace
roof above my head, avoid a civil
war, I had to stay (just formally,
you understand) aloof.

8

Orlov made me pay. He beat me
in the boudoir; buggered off with ladies' maids
and kitchen sluts. Besotted, half insane,
for thirteen years I tried to rein him in

until I found him ravishing the Princess
Golitsina. 'Fini', I cried. 'C'est trop, alors.
Enough!' He snivelled round my skirts, the dolt,
he threatened to get rough. I put my guards

on high alert, I changed the locks and bolts.
I paid him off with serfs and titles, pensions,
silverplate. He had the grace to give me,
in return, a solitaire, worth half a million

roubles. I kept it, just for old times' sake;
and entertained no scruples when I bid him
'Do svidaniya, now, goodbye.' Went off to have
a cry.

9

Casting round at forty-three to find another
man, I sent an invitation to
Vasilchikov, Lieutenant Alexander,
twenty-eight, to be my aide-de-camp.

We wined and dined together, tried it out.
My appetite was great. But he grew dull and
moody, had headaches every night, or so he
said, and soon he could not function in the

bed. I pensioned off this sulky mate with
large estates; a mansion in the city.
I set him up for life. *Et me voilà
encore une fois*: a spinster, no one's partner,

lover, wife.

Then I recalled a one-eyed lion, a wit
with dirty hair – Potemkin, Gregory,
an officer, nail-biter, mimic, balladeer,
off battling with the Turks. I wrote a little

note. He came at once. Oh I was mean!
I dangled him for one whole year in Petersburg
until he called my bluff, and in a huff
went off to join a monastery, refusing

to come out until I sent the Countess Bruce
with proof of my esteem. *Oh Gregory,*
my golden tiger, peacock, Tartar cat;
my little pigeon, Cossack, Muscovite;

my darling Grisha, sweetest friend. Restless,
after two years in my arms, he flew the coop.
I had to let him go. But not before we
secretly were wed; agreed that when

apart we could take lovers, but not give away
the heart. Potemkin would select young men
of rank to service me, have them inspected
for VD by Doctor Rogerson,

and tested for performance in the bed
by Ladies Bruce and Protasova. *But you, my hungry*

Gregory, whenever you appeared back from
the wars, half naked in your tiger-wrap,

omnipotent, a veritable God,
expected all these lesser men to move out of
the favourite's HQ which now belonged
– like me, amour – to you.

II

The trouble was I grew too fond of Peter
Zavadovsky, thirty-seven, looks to die for,
sexually green; a soldier with
a penchant for the classics. Between the sheets,

ecstatic, acrobatic, I smothered him
with kisses, gave him twenty thousand roubles
straight away. 'Petrinka, my Petruskha
Petrushinka, all will pass', I wrote

with fevered hands, 'all will pass, except
my passion for you'. I signed myself (I blush to think)
'your Katia, your Velvet Troglodyte,
your midnight Lady Dynamite'. My angel, my dear

lordling, did not like my daytime self:
the workaholic Empress Katerina:

dutiful, obsessed. From dawn to dusk
I laboured at my desk – affairs of state,

you know, and all the rest. Peter locked
himself away. 'Neglected, used, depressed,'
he said he was. I sent him off
to convalesce, with orders not to fret.

'Read Tacitus', I urged him, tongue in cheek.
Gave him a ring as pledge of future trysts.
A stricken stag, he pined for years until I snubbed him
(cruel to be kind) in Mogilev. That did the trick.

12

The very day that Petrushinka left,
I gave a trial run to Zorich, Simon.
A fiery Serb, he passed the test, but messed things up,
the fool. Absurd of him to want the sole

possession of my body, to have exclusive
rights. He picked a fight with Gregory
Potemkin. 'Come on, you prick', he jeered,
'let's have a duel', Potemkin did not blink his single

eye. He gave the lad a cauliflower
ear and threw him out.

13

The next to warm my Arctic bed was Ivan
Rimsky-Korsakov, aged twenty-four, a Horseguard
from Smolensk, of noble stock. Oh, he was such
a dish! But then I found him locked

between the thighs of Lady Bruce, my *éprouveuse*,
who should have had him only once, the witch.
I went beserk when they eloped. Drank vodka
like a fish. Had one-night stands with Stakiev

and Strakhov; with Ronstov, Levashev and even
Mordinov, the jerk!

14

Potemkin sent an officer of twenty-three,
Lanskoi, Alexander, to kiss me, calm me,
cheer me up. *Sashinka, my darling boy,*
I gave you presents, peasants, diamonds, palaces

but you just wanted books. Heir of my spirit.
Staff of my old age. I shaped you,
educated you, I taught you French. In bed you were
a sprite, your wiry torso a delight.

But you succumbed to inflammation of the throat.
Malignant. Oh my darling, oh my dote,
I nursed you like a child, stayed in your room.
I didn't sleep for days or change my clothes.

'Contagious', said the doctors, 'it's quinsy, lethal,
get her out!' But I stayed put. *You passed away*
in my embrace, worn out with aphrodisiacs
I never knew you took to keep you perked.

I went round in a haze. Applied myself to
languages. Tried Finnish, Turkish. But it didn't
work. I threw myself at vulgar studs like
Stoyanov and Miloradovich;

was like a bitch in heat with Miklashevsky.
I lost the head. I wished that I was dead.

15

Enormous, short of breath at fifty-five,
I wasn't over yet. Potemkin sent me
Alexander Yermalov, aged thirty-four,
as bedfellow and friend. This officer had

springy curls, flat nose and puffy lips.
'Vraiement a white nigger, quoi? – a little monkey,

[253]

là, extraordinaire,' the ladies teased.
Men sniggered as he passed. My bliss was not

to last. Yermalov conspired with
the enemies of state; besmirched Potemkin's
name. Forced to choose between them,
at a loss, I had to fire my paramour.

I granted him the Order of the Eagle;
awarded him four thousand serfs in Belarus;
a hundred thousand roubles (in hard cash),
a stash of silverplate.

16

As fate would have it, Mister Redcoat, Alexander
Mamonov, was waiting in the wings.
For three nights in a row he stoked my fires.
I broke with my routines. I got up late,

I gave the nod. He got the job, a team of English
horses and a jewelled walking stick. But
two years later, melancholic, sick of me
and morbid as a prisoner in a cell,

he made my life sheer hell. We played at cat and
mouse until one day he came to me in

tears, confessed his love for Princess
Sherbatova, twenty-six, and pregnant now

by him. My maid of honour, what a blow!
As usual, I was the last to know.

17

The remedy for Mamonov's deceit
was the hasty installation (after private
consultation with my confidante, the Lady
Naryshina – not with Gregory this time,

too far away, and I forgot) of Zubov, Plato,
twenty-two, the youngest of the lot.
At sixty, I was blinded by his charm,
his eyes, his quivering ringlets and his jewelled suit.

I powdered up my face, I rouged. I leaned forever
on his arm; kept him beside me morning, noon ·
and night; put up with his pet monkey
which pooed upon settees and chairs and dangled from

the chandeliers; pulled wigs off pink and balding pates,
spread fleas at an alarming rate. I think I let my
darling Plato almost run the State.
Potemkin came post-haste to Petersburg

from God knows where – the Southern colonies, perhaps,
the new frontier – to get myself and Russia back
on track.

18

He threw a party for me with three thousand guests.
And elephants, and orchestras and acrobats.
Resplendent in his uniform of red and gold,
a cloak of velvet and a diamond clasp,

he wore a hat so loaded down with precious stones,
he could not bear it on his head for long,
but had a page-boy carry it instead.
We drank from Persian goblets, dined off golden

plates on oysters, veal and mutton; beef;
on dark Crimean grapes. But when at 2
a.m. I took my leave, with Plato Zubov
glued to my silk sleeve, Potemkin knelt

before me, kissed my hand, my hem, my orthopaedic
shoes, my bits and bobs, broke into sobs.
I sighed. I nearly cried. I stroked his head. I said
'Adieu'. In six months he was dead.

19

Zubov's power was complete. He had the country
crawling at his feet. Though I was sixty-
seven now and had no teeth, I did not see
myself as old and weak. My heartbeat was

irregular, my legs so swollen I could hardly
walk. In court and corridor I heard them
talk: 'It's dropsy, dissipation, the old
whore. What else could you expect?'

But I refused to be put out. Wrote in my diary
'Merry as a lark'. Drank coffee by the
bucketful, and peppered wine from Spain
to cure the gout. I rose at six and rubbed my face

with ice, in the old way. And worked a ten-hour
day. By night I petted Zubov, curled his
hair; read Montesquieu and Diderot,
Voltaire.

20

A shooting star streaked through the sky at Tsarskoye
Selo. 'That's not for me', I told myself.
Then lightning struck a tree. I called my *femme
de chambre* at once. Rushed to the WC.

21

She found me slumped and foaming at the mouth.
I'd had a stroke. The doctor, though he knew it was
a waste of time, applied a single leech.
Placed mustard plasters on my marbled feet.

But I remained unconscious, quite remote.
With great big rattles in my throat, I died.
The snow in Petersburg was falling down.
Some people knelt and prayed. Some people cried.

FOUR POEMS IN PROGRESS

BEDS

Italian beds *are*
wall to wall
~~sure~~ there's no end
to them at all.

English beds *are*
soft ~~precise and~~ deep ;
designed exclusively
for sleep.

Irish beds
know their place
they let the weather
set the pace.

But Spanish beds ~~are~~ , *the ~~modern~~ issue*
are ~~corridas,~~ bull-rings,
flamenco, vino , ~~tiss twio,~~
midnight flings.

Dorothy Carpenter

Beds

Italian beds are
wall to wall
There seems no end
to them at all.

English beds are
soft and deep;
designed exclusively
for sleep.

Irish beds
know their place
they let the weather
set the pace.

But Spanish beds
are bull-rings;
flamenco, vino,
midnight flings.

[Coming up out of the sea]

Coming up out of the sea
the slither and slur
A flick of my tail to propel me
A blur of silver grey
my wet fur.

Coming up out of the sea
the wallow and weed
finding my feet: the beat
of my heels on the ground, the
shedding of gills.

Coming up out of the sea
the liquid and lurch
leaving the dreams like phantom
boats high in the bay
resuming my shape

Coming up out of the sea
the liquid and lurch
dazzled by light
returning at night
down the slip or the mica-strewn
steps
(or: the cold granite steps)
Leaving the dreams, like boats,
phantom boats, high in the bay
stepping out, climbing up cold granite steps
to the dazzle of day.

[A holy man one day at half-past three]

A holy man one day at half-past three
Encroached his hand beneath my childish smock
Forced me to awkward sit upon his knee.

'We'll be best friends', he, smiling, said to me
And took me from my brother to a rock
A holy man one day at half-past three.

'If you will show me yours, then mine you'll see'
'Oh No!', I cried, but he ignored my shock
Forced me to awkward sit upon his knee.

He groped for breasts where my small flat chest be
Breathed down my neck and fiddled with his cock
A holy man one day at half-past three.

'I'm still too young', I gasped, but he my plea
Ignored again and held me in a lock
Forced me to awkward sit upon his knee.

I'll never know what made him set me free*
His hands fell limp, I smoothed down my frock
A holy man one day at half-past three
Forced me to awkward sit upon his knee.

*My angel guardian fought to set me free
or: My mother's prayers at home stopped tragedy

[We found the hives among the orange-trees]

We found the hives among the orange-trees
Abandoned by the swarms, like wooden tombs
In time there will be honeycombs and bees.

We walked the sun-baked track in dungarees
The black ants crawled out of their catacombs
We found the hives among the orange-trees.

Inside the boxes, waxy filigrees
And corpses, ghostly moths and fractured looms
In time there will be honeycombs and bees.

Our love was white and powdery as the breeze
(or:
The earth was white and powdery in the breeze)
Had almost blown away in tiny spumes
(or:
And wild birds all displayed their tiny plumes)
We found the hives among the orange-trees

We turned away and felt a great unease
(or:
The mystery grew around the absentees)
Where was the honey-man who built these wombs?
In time there will be honeycombs and bees.

I dream of furry queens, the droney groom
(or:
Where were the furry queens, the droney grooms?)
How long to wait until the orange blooms?
We found the hives among the orange-trees
In time there will be honeycombs and bees.

NOTES

Notes on the Edition

Dorothy Molloy was born in Ballina, Co. Mayo in 1942. She first visited Spain and Catalonia – for which she developed an abiding love – while studying languages at University College Dublin; for some years after graduation, she was employed by UCD to work in Spanish provincial archives unearthing and deciphering documents connected with the 'Wild Geese' – Irish soldiers who had served in continental armies in the seventeenth and eighteenth centuries. She moved to Barcelona in the 1960s where she worked as an art critic, journalist and painter, winning several prizes for her own paintings and drawings. In 1980 she returned to Ireland where she further developed her interest in languages, editing medieval texts in Catalan and Castilian for her MPhil and PhD degrees. After her marriage in 1983, she continued her involvement with painting and poetry, and began teaching creative writing. She thrived in the critical, supportive atmosphere of the Thornfield Poets writing group in Dublin. A draft typescript of poems, *Hare Soup*, was accepted for publication by Faber & Faber in the autumn of 2002, and completed in the summer of 2003; tragically, Dorothy had been diagnosed with cancer at the end of that year and died in the week that finished copies arrived from the printers, in January 2004. *Hare Soup* received glowing reviews, and was followed by two further books, *Gethsemane Day* and *Long-distance Swimmer*, containing material drawn from her papers and published in 2006 and 2009. Those collections are represented in this edition in full.

Dorothy wrote for many hours each day in the last few years of her life, often selecting phrases or images from her extensive 'free writing' and working on them until they satisfied her as poems. The present volume adds to the three volumes of her published poetry with a selection of forty previously unpublished poems taken from the Dorothy Molloy Carpenter archive in the National Library of Ireland. It selects from only those new pieces that had achieved a recognisable degree of finish and that seemed worthy of wider readership. As Dorothy rarely recorded composition dates, these pieces are ordered alphabetically, while 'The loneliness of Catherine the Great' has been treated discretely because she considered it as a piece of independent standing. In some cases, lineation and punctuation suggest that Dorothy might have given the texts further attention, had she lived; where these poems were untitled in typescript, the edition follows her frequent practice of adopting a first-line title. The archive also holds a number of poems in progress that could not be considered finished but which are nonetheless interesting, four of which are included here. It is hoped that the sample of new material will encourage scholars to delve deeper into the archive, and I would like to thank the staff in the NLI and Dr Luz Mar Gonzáles-Arias for their help in locating this material. I would also like to thank Dorothy's agent, Jonathan Williams, and Jessie Lendennie and Salmon Poetry for permission to republish *Long-distance Swimmer*. Finally, I would like to thank Matthew Hollis, who helped me to assemble this volume at Faber & Faber.

Dorothy's commitment to writing and to poetry is apparent from her 'Credo', which was found in the notebook beside her bed when she died and which is printed at the beginning of this book, and in the following note she wrote to herself on 4 September 2002:

'I see my poems as little models that I make every day – little, precise objects.'

ANDREW CARPENTER
Dublin, Spring 2019

Notes on the Poems

'Dream': *cruci dum spiro fido* ('while I live I trust in the Cross') is the motto of Dorothy's school, Loreto Abbey, Dalkey.

'S.O.S.': the St John of God Hospital provides help for those suffering mental or emotional problems.

'Going your own way': the Kish is a lighthouse in Dublin Bay.

'Alcossebre': Alcossebre is a small seaside town between Barcelona and Valencia. Patufet is a very small child who appears in Catalan folktales. To prevent himself being trodden on, he sings, 'patim, patam, patum'. However, he is eaten by a cow and when his parents call out, 'Where are you?', he replies that he is 'in the cow's belly where it neither snows nor rains'.

'For Bracken (3 months' mind)': Bracken and Duke were golden retrievers owned by Dorothy.

Index of Titles and First Lines

Poem titles are in italics. First lines are roman.